These
Stories
I Lived

Growing Up on a Plantation Farm in South Georgia

HAZEL JUANITA WINTERS COLLINS

authorHOUSE®

AuthorHouse™
1663 Liberty Drive
Bloomington, IN 47403
www.authorhouse.com
Phone: 1 (800) 839-8640

Published by AuthorHouse 06/29/2017

ISBN: 978-1-5246-9304-6 (sc)
ISBN: 978-1-5246-9302-2 (hc)
ISBN: 978-1-5246-9303-9 (e)

Library of Congress Control Number: 2017908086

Print information available on the last page.

FOREWORD

These stories by Hazel Juanita Winters Collins will take you back to a time of the horse and buggy, the early automobile, pre-refrigeration, moonshine, and the one-room schoolhouse. For this was the time of Ms. Collins' youth, a time when she was between the ages of five and thirteen, the period 1924 to 1932. From recollections in her mature years we learn about the many people she knew and grew up with on her parents' plantation farm in South Georgia: parents Ruth and Clower, sisters Claudene and Sarah, black Irish "Aunt Min," a specially gifted child named "Angel," uncles Clarence and Willis, cousins Epp, Ellick, Junior and Frances, and the many black people she loved and admired: Isabella and Allen, "Uncle" Gus and "Aunt" Mary, Mousie and Ed, Sugar, Alice, Lizzer and "Uncle" Alp. Then there were the Bruces who arrived from New York City. Like "Uncle" Gus and "Aunt" Mary before them, and Mousie and Ed later, they took up residence at the Creek House, and for the year they were there, sons Ben, Bo and Boaz got into so much trouble for their lack of knowledge about undomesticated animals, it might have spelled their doom had the family not decided to pick up stakes and return to the city of the four million.[1]

Not least of Juanita's many memories is "Grandpa Bill,"

---

[1]   As O'Henry called it two decades earlier.

in actuality her Great-Grandfather William Edmondson, who died when she was eleven. Two of her fifteen stories regard him directly and several others mention him in passing. Truly, one might estimate he was her favorite and indeed, we are given the impression his promise of God allowing his return from the grave in "Grandpa Bill the Ghost," was fulfilled. What I can say from personal experience is that through her declining years Ms. Collins continued to mention him as if he were among the living.

Reading Ms. Collins' original draft was like finding rare gems needing only the polisher's wheel. Take for example, the description of when she thought she was going to get a switching after returning from Uncle Willis' dry-goods store in "Mousie's Getting Married":

> I did not have to go far to find mamma. She came bounding up the stairs shouting "Young lady!" to bring the house down. "Young lady" was the expression used for all little girls on our farm just before they were given a switching that was supposed to last a lifetime.

Or again, in the very next passage:

> … when mamma shouted, "Young Lady!," I braced for the gallberry switch. But mamma glanced at the material on the cutting board and curiosity got the better of her. Or was it her love of beautiful things?

That image of impending doom contrasted with tenderness for things beautiful is itself an image of beauty and wonder. And it is an added wonder we are seeing this through the mind of a woman who was remembering this event 60 years later, feeling the privilege of being witness to what we could never see in our own lives, for the style of life that then existed has long faded from the American scene. In this sense it is history. Not Dr. Wellsley's History, not something we could learn in school, because these are common, even trivial episodes in the life of one family, but history nevertheless because it is part of the human drama occurring within the larger fabric of human existence.

Pearl S. Buck believed the truest stories are those that come from the people, and she meant by this not only the ordinary people, but people of the land as opposed to people from the cities. Hazel Juanita Winters Collins was a "down home" but more than ordinary person from the land of the South and I invite you with heartfelt sincerity to read her plain and simple stories. Simple as they are they bespeak something beautiful, but also something true.

D.D.Desjardins

TABLE OF CONTENTS

ADVENTURER, EXPLORER, SETTLER

When James Edward Oglethorpe left England in 1733 to settle a colony for King George II, my ancestors were most likely with him.

Oglethorpe was elected to Parliament in 1722 due to his distinction in the campaign against the Turks. While in Parliament, he learned about the suffering and hardship of those who had gone to prison for their debts. He was given the opportunity to persuade these prisoners to accompany him to a new land, thus gaining their freedom and a pardoning of their debts. This effort on behalf of insolvent debtors brought about the colonization of Georgia.

So it was! Freed prisoners and their families helped settle the state of Georgia.

My great-grandfather was a clock maker. We still have one of his clocks today. And from the stories I've heard, it appears he was crusty enough to borrow money to own a business even if he couldn't repay the loan.

How did his ancestors find "The Land of the Trembling Earth?" Did Oglethorpe help families to settle this particular area or did the settlers find their own part of Georgia? Oglethorpe, I believe, was busy in the Savannah area. I therefore think great-grandpa's ancestors and the other settlers might have stumbled upon this lush, rich place on their own. I'm sure the people who settled in the flat lands of South Georgia, the area around which Valdosta is to be found today, must have gazed in wonder when they first laid eyes upon this place. The rich wet-lands with their abundance of berries, plant foods and all species of wildlife, even little brown bears, made each tomorrow a new adventure. Not to mention the beautiful, clear running rivers. Once discovered, there was a love for this land that continued from generation to generation.

The Okefinoke swamp was not too many miles from the area where great-grandfather's ancestors settled. Their hard work, perseverance, and the rearing of large families helped settle Georgia. "My grandpa, Ol' Man Oss," as he was called, remarked that great-grandpa would declare to anyone who would listen, "This new world we have come upon is a wonderful world!"

We were taught to "Never Forget" that our ancestors who came out of the prisons of England were entrepreneurs, not criminals. I suppose this teaching was not a bad idea because many times the feeling we Georgia folks were a good people helped us pick a full sack of cotton when we might have gotten away with picking a smaller amount. We worked harder knowing we were quality people!

I think one of the first opinions I arrived at was all my relatives and everyone I knew, for that matter, had a lot of pride in themselves. I have noticed people from South Georgia, particularly, appear to have big egos. All of them, including myself, talk as if we know everything. When a South Georgia native, white or black, starts talking, he probably does know what his is talking about, or he wouldn't be talking.

My father became the owner and operator of the old farm where he was reared, as was his father before him. It was now his job to maintain order and provide for the family. And there were a lot of us! A big old farmhouse was our home. There was "Ol' Man Oss," my grandpa, and my beautiful grandmother who everyone called "Miss Delia." Her name was Ardelia, I think, which was cut to "Delia." Miss "Delia" didn't come to the new country on the same boat since she was not English. She was different, and always dressed properly as a lady should. She had eight children whom she taught to take their rightful place in the world, including my mother. She and mother seemed busy all the time but as I look back, in all honesty, I think about all they did was have children.

The farm and all its activities will always remain in my memory. When thinking of those times, I thank God for the opportunities I had to appreciate and respect all people and creatures. Life on any farm during the turn of the century was hard. Black and white folks worked side by side. The old and the young, the black and the white, we people who worked together knew we could not survive without each other. We loved the black people who lived on our farm. It was Sugar, a little black woman, who reared me. She taught, "Thou shalt not kill." Today, I do not kill anything. If there is an ant in my house, I pick him up and put him outside. And I think of Sugar. If there is a snake in my yard, the yard man and I allow him safe passage. We do not kill him. And I think of Sugar. This tiny black woman who was responsible for my care taught me many things, among which, kindness and tolerance.

My father was a tall, quiet man with bright blue eyes and curly black hair. He went about the place overseeing the work that was always going on. I never heard him raise his voice in anger to anyone. And I never saw him get riled up. He was always so calm.

Most of the people who worked the farm had been on our place all their lives. I remember Gar and Isabella who had a little girl they called "Deuce." And I also remember Alan and Sugar, who didn't have any children. There were usually five families on our farm and most of them stayed with us all their lives. But it wasn't easy to keep a good black family. The neighboring farmers would coax them away by offering more benefits, more money, and better housing. But really, the money was not as important as the benefits and housing. Nobody had money! All land owners could offer housing, and benefits like health-care and food, but very little money.

We grew plenty of food on our farm and all of us ate the same food. We raised turkeys, chickens, and ducks. We also raised our own beef and pork. And everybody could go fishing on Saturdays. Not to mention there were plenty of vegetables.

I suppose our only money crop was cotton. And the cotton patch is where all the little black children and all the little white children learned to know each other. And learned to love or hate each other, too.

My two best friends were Mousie and Alice. Their mother and father were John and Mary, but I do not remember their last name. Mousie and Alice were the best friends I ever had. They always hid me from the wrath of my sisters and loved me in spite of me.

The stories in this book are true experiences of the way we lived and the way we got along together. My memory serves me well and I am happy to remember such a time, so long ago.

THE DEMON AT
OUR PICNIC

It brings tears of happiness to my eyes as I recall hurrying home from school one fine day to find a lot of excitement all about the place. Everyone was hurrying this way and that, so excited and happy!

Mousie and Alice, my two little black friends – and a very real part of our farm – filled me in on the activities. "We're all goin' for a swim in the river and then we're goin' to have a picnic right there on the river bank!" Mousie was shouting at me.

"Oh," I said. I knew we must have finished hoeing peanuts or gotten the cotton picked or something. The completion of some farm project was usually the reason for us getting a swim and a picnic, which also included bringing our cats and dogs and all our friends.

Little black children and little white children gathered up their homemade swimsuits in anticipation of playing in the warm river water. Our farm was only about three miles away. So once we got started, it wasn't long before we were all in the broad, slowly moving water splashing about and having a good time. That is, everyone except the adults, who were loaded down with vittles and all the implements for our picnic.

Oh, what a day! I shall never forget the beauty of the water;

water so clear one could see everywhere and watch the tiny, little fish scurrying about on the bright, sandy carpet of the river's bottom. Even those of us who were very young realized the waterways of Southern Georgia were full of fascination and excitement.

All too soon, we were called to the picnic, spread out on a knoll type area beside the river bank. The knoll looked as if it had been used before as a picnic table. The top was rounded and low at the sides, which made it just right for the smaller children. Nevertheless, one particular mother had trouble getting her child to sit at this strange table. He simply refused to stay. I wonder now whatever happened to this little boy. For it seems to me he was psychic.

When as many of us could be settled around the knoll as were able, and all others found places where they might, the food was served and we all commenced eating. But the little boy and his mother sat apart, for he still refused to go near the knoll.

Once everyone had eaten and the dishes were collected, the children began playing on the knoll, enjoying themselves. All except the little boy and me, for, as mother used to say, I only played when I was all dressed up, and on this day I wasn't. So instead I watched the other children play, which lasted until the sun was going down, for nobody wanted to leave.

Suddenly, there was a tremor and a slight movement of the earth beneath us. Every eye flew wide open. Then everyone became immobile. Mousie and Alice, with their beautiful black eyes, very expressive when speaking, spoke to me now the word "help!" Gar, their father, reacted immediately. So did my father. Gar began yelling, "Get them chillen outta here!," while daddy snatched children off the knoll shouting for all the mothers to do likewise. All obeyed and began getting their children away from the river.

My poor mother was so shocked and frightened she didn't know what to do. Not at first, that is. Soon, however, she began picking up her silver and china. So while daddy carried me off to safety, mother was attempting to salvage the family heirloom. It is an irony we were too poor to afford paper cups and plates but the silver and china, having been passed down through generations, is what we brought to our picnics.

About this time the most thunderous roar came from the heaving, trembling earth. Everyone was screaming, scampering, and skidaddling, trying to keep from falling in the river or being carried to heaven by the moving earth pushed up by some roaring demon!

Daddy and Gar were helping everyone, trying to get them headed toward home. In the process, daddy tried to inform us what was going on. "Hurry, everyone – no time to loose. You are hearing a bull alligator calling for his mate! Soon, every gator in Georgia will be converging on this spot!"

And that was the end of our picnic.

Now the years have passed and daddy and Gar are gone. But something still bothers me. I would like to have asked: why did you wait so long to tell us the demon under the river bank was an alligator? Had you told us sooner, we might have been more cooperative. We might have headed home sooner and maybe even beaten you there. In fact, I think we did anyway!

At the age of six, I knew I had heard the mating call of the alligator and would never forget it. It was a frightening experience I suppose, but I do not recall being overly afraid. I think I was moreover excited. For somehow at that early age I began to realize every living creature had his own place in the world. And I somehow became aware the alligator tried just as hard as we did to live in peace with his surroundings. For example, I once remember seeing a huge alligator lying submerged in the river for hours with only his eyes and nostrils showing. We children were playing nearby and I thought at the time the gator didn't really want to scare us, but merely enjoyed watching us. Somehow I was not afraid even though I knew the gator could slap us across Georgia with his huge tail if he wanted to. But he didn't want to; he only wanted his place, and some peace to go with it.

MEAT, MEAL AND LARD

Saturday was always a special day on our farm. The various children would gather, laughing and playing, knowing all the while they had come for a particular chore. They came running just after daybreak, some with their parents following a little behind, perhaps a dozen in all, knowing my father would be at the back steps of our house to greet them. This was as much a social event as it was an important means of support for our farm families. These children, both black and white, had always lived on our farm with their parents, who toiled the fields and raised our animals. Sometimes referred to as "sharecroppers," the parents did many of the things that had to be done in the days before heavy machinery took the toil out of making farms a viable enterprise. And I think back now to how special each child was, as if one of our own.

While father waited for all to be present and accounted for, the children would begin playing hop-scotch, tag and other games. But eventually, when all were present, they would form a line and my father would begin by asking, "What can I do for you, Mary?" or "What have you come for, Johnny?" And each child would reply in their laughing, little voices: "Meat, meal and lard, Missuh Clowa," which was the best their tiny mouths could utter regarding

"Mister," or father's name, "Clower." Father would by now be standing at the edge of the porch behind a large marble-topped table that mamma normally used for setting out her potted plants. Now, however, it was cleared and washed and over-layed with oil-cloth on which various foodstuffs were arranged.

The meal was home-made from the corn we raised, ground in our own mill. And before the corn ever went to the mill it had to be shucked and run through a corn-sheller. The shucks themselves were dried and used to stuff mattresses. The corn on the other hand we passed though the sheller, which was hand-cranked and removed the kernels from the cob. Altogether it was a week's work, with thousands of ears processed each day, enough by week's end to produce a decent-sized land-fill. Most of the spent cobs, however, we used for kindling. The kernels were funneled directly into a "crusher" which in actuality was a grinding mill operated like the sheller, that is, by hand.

As to the lard, it was rendered from the fat and meat trimmings of our hogs, after cutting away the edible portions, the bacon, ham hock, ribs and backbone. These pieces of fat and meat trimmings were put into large iron pots and cooked, producing a liquefied fat that was poured through cheese-cloth into large jars that, once full, were sealed and allowed to cool. The cooling caused the fat to solidify into what we called "lard." Sealed properly, the shelf-life, even during the warmer months of summer, was good enough that the lard never turned rancid and was edible all through the year.

The meat was the most cherished of the allotment and consisted of lamb and goat in the Spring, turkey in the Fall, and beef, chicken and pork nearly all year round. The beef, lamb and goat, because they were unsalted, were only served fresh, whereas the pork and turkey were cured - and sometimes smoked - and could be served long after their initial preparation.

The smokehouse was where we cured the hog meat and turkey, a building of wood with concrete floors about the size of an average kitchen. The floor was built with a pit area into which we placed huge oak logs that were set ablaze, then soon extinguished, to where the logs merely smoldered. Burning this way, they produced a thick, heavy smoke that saturated the meat hanging from the rafters, the smoke regulated by, and exiting, a small chimney at the top of the ceiling.

This was but one of the ways in which meat was preserved in the days before refrigeration. For beef, lamb, goat and chicken, meats that typically were not smoked, there was what was called an "ice-house." The "ice-house" was a structure unto itself, near to, but apart from, our home, with a floor of loose-fitting boards over pine-straw to allow drainage. Every other day, wagons from town brought huge blocks of ice that were placed on this floor, and the meats were placed on top to keep them cool. Regardless, no meat was ever kept this way very long. For the usual custom was to share freshly slaughtered meat with neighboring farms, the understanding being they, in turn, would share their meat with us. With the introduction of refrigerators, this neighborly practice eventually died away. But during the time I am speaking, we were still using an ice-house and our tenant farmers, who had no refrigeration of their own, depended on us for fresh meat. This meat distribution actually occurred twice a week, both Saturday mornings and mid-week.

The several children who lined up in front of father's marble-topped table each Saturday – but not Wednesday, for that was a school day - didn't necessarily understand the toil and labor that went into making the food that stood there, only that their parents, who did understand and had done the work to produce it, sent them for their portion to last through the week. Their little part, duly instructed, was merely to reply to what father would ask, and say it they did with unfailing repetition: "Meat, meal and lard, Missuh Clowa, meat, meal and lard!"

THE COOLING BOARD

I knew all about cooling boards very early in life. Being reared on a big farm in South Georgia with lots of people and animals – seeing the things that went on – you knew everything by the time you were still young. In fact, when the Granny woman delivered me, I realized almost immediately I had better take charge of my life or someone might send me back!

And so one of my earliest recollections involves the cooling board. My memory about it is still rather vivid. For example, I remember the room where the cooling board was located. It was back of the farmhouse nearest the creek. A long porch ran the length of our house and a deep well had been dug at the far end. The well had been dug so we could fetch water at night without leaving the safety of our home.

At night, rattlesnakes often slithered up onto the warm steps leading to the porch. They loved warm places and if someone decided to sleep on the porch during the hot months of summer, chances are they'd have a rattlesnake cuddled next to them by morning. Fortunately, I always managed to avoid the cuddling. We respected the rattlesnake enough that we didn't try to wake him. And I suppose he respected us enough to never come into the house. Anyway, this was the way things were in South Georgia and the reason it was necessary to place the well at the far end of the porch.

The cooling board was also a necessary part of life on the

farm, or most anywhere, I suppose, a hundred or so years ago. I was just a little girl the first time I saw it used but the sight of it made a lasting impression. For example, I recall it was handmade of beautiful yellow pine, and was the length of a normal bed, wide enough for one person. A soft white sheet covered the polished surface and a thin feather pillow with a nice muslin case rested at the head. The cooling board itself rested on two strong "wooden horses" - saw horses, as I believe they are called today.

By now you will realize the cooling board was intended for the recently departed. After a person died, the body was bathed and arranged on the board, not to be touched by anyone else until the body was beautifully straight. For no one wanted their loved one to go to heaven sick and old-looking.

The body was placed on the cooling board before rigor mortis set in. The head of the person was placed on the pillow perfectly straight. When the cooling process was complete, the person would be dressed and ready for their journey. No longer would they be old and bent, now they would walk into heaven straight and erect. And they would wear their best suit of clothes, too; that is, if they had a suit. If they didn't, someone always donated one.

Once the person was bathed, arranged and properly clothed, the cooling board had done its job, but it was never put away. It was instead adorned with another white sheet and fresh pillow case for the next person.

Not everyone in the community owned a cooling board. So we loaned ours from time to time. Most of the time, we loaned the room, too.

The first time I saw ours used I think I was about six years of age.

We had a black man on our place called "Uncle Alp." He had lived with us as far back as I can remember. In fact, we inherited Uncle Alp when we inherited the farm. He was the best thing we got out of the whole deal. He worked on the farm when my grandfather owned the place and continued there after grandfather died. He cut wood for our many fireplaces. Daddy and some of the other men would saw the trees down and saw the core into blocks. Uncle Alp would then split the blocks into the right sizes for our cook stoves and fireplaces.

Uncle Alp worked as a woodman summer and winter. The little black children and the little white children loved Uncle Alp. We took him cool water and food as often as we could steal it from the kitchen.

One morning, Uncle Alp came for breakfast. While waiting to be called by the cook, he sat down in a rocking chair and died. All the blacks and whites came running. Most of us were crying. We all loved him.

Daddy called several men by name to help prepare Uncle Alp for the cooling board. Those who were not afraid to handle a dead body hurriedly came and undressed Uncle Alp, then washed and positioned him. In this way Uncle Alp would be straight and tall when he entered heaven, not bent and crooked as he was in life.

The neighbors came, both black and white, to pay their respects. It was customary, especially on the farms, to hold a wake.

We had a neighbor, a known moonshiner, who lived by the river. He had two sons. One had long yellow curls and the other, long black curls. They were probably in their mid-twenties, both good-looking, and their father was proud of them. It didn't matter they didn't have a lick of sense. In fact, I don't know whether the father could even tell if anything was wrong with them. Where he got those boys was anyone's guess, for it didn't seem there was a mamma in the family.

Anyway, the family made moonshine, and brought some for the wake. When they arrived, they first went to see Uncle Alp. I suppose they'd never seen anyone on a cooling board before. Then father and sons returned to the porch where all the other men were gathered. The moonshine was passed around many times and the party was on!

Meanwhile, father and those helping him placed Uncle Alp in the casket they had made for him. They then placed the casket in the visiting area.

The boy with the blond hair had by now drunk about all the moonshine he could hold and was wandering around looking for a place to sleep. He wandered into the cooling room – and seeing the cooling board, which he was too drunk to recognize – decided to stretch out, pulling the sheet over his head. In just a little while, his brother, who was also pretty drunk, walked down the porch and passed the cooling board just as Goldie-Locks was turning over. Brother let out a shriek and bounded down the porch. Landing on the well-curbing, he must have thought he was still on the porch, so he jumped again. There was no mistaking the splash he made as he landed in the water. And of course everyone heard the scream he let out when he thought he saw a raising of the dead. So those who were sober came running and pulled the boy out of the well, plopping him belly first onto the porch. Almost immediately, he began vomiting water and moonshine all over the place. Handsome as he was, the image of him getting sick this way did nothing for his appearance. And the fact he was drunk was no excuse either.

For years afterward, especially when the cooling board was in use, the story was repeated how Goldie-Locks' brother made a fool of himself being frightened by a ghost!

As for Uncle Alp, he entered heaven straight and erect – and no doubt with a smile on his face, too.

The cooling board remained with us for many years, and was used every so often. Then, I don't know just when, it disappeared. To this day I believe our undertaker borrowed and never returned it. But I never asked because, being a teenager by then, I was glad it was gone. To tell the truth, all the time it was there, I avoided the cooling room whenever possible. For it was a sad reminder of all the good people who had passed away, and those whose time was yet to come. I never got over the feeling there might be one more member of our large family getting straightened and prepared for their long journey into heaven.

GRANDPA BILL AND THE
WATER-MOCCASINS

The sun was shining brightly this late September morning as grandpa and I walked down to inspect the rice patch.

I loved the old man dearly and it was the highlight of my young years (I was then about five years old) to be allowed to follow him around. He was a big man with a red face, blue eyes and black hair. I believe his bright eyes and angular features were definite signs of his being an Englishman. In fact, I think grandpa's grandfather must have been one of those persons who came from the prisons of England. For if you remember your history, James Oglethorpe became a colonist after getting permission from Parliament to settle a colony in the New World.[2] Unable to attract volunteers, he negotiated with the prison system on behalf of prisoners with unpaid debts. His plan was to give debtors their freedom if they and their families would settle in Georgia. And this, I believe, is how my ancestors first came to the New World.

As we walked, grandpa told me his plans and I acted like I knew what he was talking about. I loved this relationship even if I didn't understand all he was saying.

---

[2]   The first settlement in this last of the British colonies in America was made at Savannah in 1733 under the personal supervision of James Oglethorpe.

For instance, one of his most frequent but hard to understand expressions was, "I bane gon do that." Eventually, I learned this meant "I have been going to do that." To tell the truth, grandfather spoke as if he had a sinus problem. I think most full-blooded Englishmen have this problem, something quite natural to the shape of their noses.

Although I sensed grandpa was not always operating in the middle of the road, he was certainly a live wire if ever there was one. Our neighboring farmers would often come to visit, ostensibly to get his advice, but more often, I believe, just to hear him speak.

On this particular day, grandpa and I were on our way to see if the rice patch was ready to be pulled and planted for the following Spring. We had a low area on our farm that held several feet of water. And if we had a wet Spring, there was usually a nice crop of rice.

If you are from Georgia and read this, you may think there was never any rice grown in our state unless possibly Savannah. But I'm here to tell you there was at least one other area where rice was grown and that was on our farm just outside Morven.[3]

Morven, in South Georgia, was about seven miles north of Valdosta. Our farm had rich soil that was often bathed by a runaway river. This particular Spring brought lots of rain and so our rice crop was bountiful. By now, however, the grains had already been gathered. The kernels were cleaned and spread out to dry, the hulls and other residue blown away by an old bellows type apparatus. Grandpa's patch usually produced enough rice for everyone. The rice was brown, not polished,

---

[3] History tells us that before the Civil War, Georgia and the Carolinas were the only states in the union where rice was grown to any great extent. Following the Civil War, however, South Carolina and Georgia abandoned rice and production shifted to Louisiana, Texas, Arkansas and California. By the 1920's, the period in question, Georgia's rice production had indeed become minimal.

and I never knew there was any other kind but brown rice until I went to college.

At first, grandpa was pleased with what he saw. The rice plants were waving in the shimmering water, about six inches above the surface. So on this day he decided to pull the plants, divide, and re-plant them for the following year. These plants would later come up when the rains began in early Spring. All this work had to be done with three or four feet of water covering the area to be planted.

But we didn't reckon on water-moccasins. The water-moccasins usually left by this time when the water got cold. Where they went I never knew. One day they were everywhere in the creeks and rivers and the next, they were gone until Spring. They were not a dangerous snake, for they had no fangs. But they did have a bite and were fierce fighters. They could take a chunk out of you if they bit you. But most of the time they stayed out of your way unless you came across a lot of them. Then you stayed out of their way!

As grandpa and I drew closer to the rice field, he suddenly became angry. His face grew red, or I should say, redder than it usually was, which was something quite amazing.

"Just look," he yelled. "They're still here!"

I looked where he was pointing. The sunlight picked up several bright dots flickering about in the water – pairs of bright dots close together, fluttering this way and that. That's all I could make out. But grandpa recognized the bright dots for what they were. He hurriedly unrolled his buggy whip and began slicing the water this way and that. Then I saw that each little pair of dots had a water-moccasin attached to it.

"They should be gone by now!" grandpa fumed.

He then gave me the scare of my life. For he walked right up to the water's edge. I thought he was going in after the snakes! But grandpa had more smarts than most people gave him credit for. And it sure helped he was an expert with that ol' buggy whip! He stood there what seemed forever slicing the water. Meanwhile, frightened by all his flailing, I backed away.

Suddenly, grandpa put his whip down. He had gotten over being angry. In fact, as we walked home, he seemed pleased about something.

It was not till next morning, however, that grandpa called all the able-bodied men, telling them to get ready to plant rice. "What did you say, pa?" asked my father. He was under the impression the moccasins were still in the rice patch. With a happy grin, grandpa told him, "I've got my rice patch back!"

Sure enough, when daddy and the others reached the rice patch, they found quite a few dead snakes, thanks to grandpa's whip.

The snakes that survived skedaddled to Winter quarters, or wherever they went by mid-Fall. For it was obvious no more little bright dots were fluttering about in the water.

On that day the rice was planted and later I watched throughout the long winter days hoping to see the rice patch turn green. And to be perfectly honest, I was happy when I noticed the little bright dots swimming around in the water again.

I think grandpa was happy, too. For he got out his buggy whip and set it aside for our next planting.

ON TRIAL FOR ATTEMPTED MURDER AT THE AGE OF SEVEN

When I was growing up in South Georgia, life was a "floating down the river" experience. Some days, everything floated along smoothly. But other days, a small child didn't have a chance. I was getting ready to experience the latter situation one morning when I walked into our huge dining-room kitchen.

All farmhouses in South Georgia had large rooms used for just about everything. I recall all the rooms in our house having fireplaces, wall to wall beds, and clothes hanging on all the walls. There were actually more rooms and space than our family needed. But with all the cats and dogs, and sometimes other peoples' children, we easily managed to fill up the space in no time!

Aside from my mother and father, I had four sisters. Most of the time, it was a fun place. Isabella, a tall, pretty black woman, took care of our kitchen. In addition, she helped us fasten our clothes and gave us breakfast before the school bus came.

Claudene, my oldest sister, was Isabella's pet. In fact, Claudene was everybody's pet. She was the first grandchild on both sides of the family - and Lordy - was she a mess!

Anyway, here I was, a tiny little girl just seven years old but already in the third grade. I started school a year early because Claudene needed a companion.

Claudene was a big girl and I never got big enough to hold my own against her unless I got someone – or something – to help me. I soon learned I had to use my brain as well as my brawn or I couldn't win.

One particular morning when I came to breakfast, there stood Claudene in my new dress, pulling out a chair to sit down. Just as she was about to sit, I ran up and snatched the chair out from under her. Wham! She hit the floor, bursting my new dress as she fell. But she also managed to hit the back of her head on the chair. Great Scott!!! Mother and Isabella nearly ran into each other trying to pick up the little darling. For a moment, I thought I had gone overboard. It looked as if I was really in for it this time!

Sugar, a little black woman I was devoted to, was hiding behind the door. She was sweet and kind to everyone. She loved me, but like me, wasn't big enough to get into a fight.

I suppose the racket woke Uncle Clarence. He came running from one of the bedrooms. There was one thing about Uncle Clarence that got everyone's attention: he was big as a battleship! I remember him so well – so big, so good-looking, and so kind. We children loved him dearly. I recall one Christmas he sent a huge box to my sisters and me. The box was filled with silk panties! We had never even seen silk panties before. Our underwear had always been homemade. Well, there were enough silk panties in that box for everyone, including Mousie, Alice, Isabella and Sugar. I plan to seek out Uncle Clarence when I get to heaven, for I know he is there.

This particular morning when I was about to get killed, Uncle Clarence brought things to order. The fact he was a lawyer meant nothing to us at the time. But before my ordeal was over, I moved him right next to the Lord himself!

Being the granddaughter of a Methodist preacher, I had been introduced to God at an early age. But religion was not working for me too well right now. Uncle Clarence, at least, was giving me some feeling of hope. He was standing between me and everyone who wanted to hurt me. When Uncle Clarence told everyone to be quiet, you could hear a pin drop.

I inched closer to the big man as he asked, "What's going on here?" At this, everyone started talking all at once. The gist of what mother and Isabella were trying to tell him was, "Juanita tried to kill Claudene." At this, I tugged at uncle's shirt sleeve to get his attention. Although he didn't address me, he put his hand on top of my head, which felt good. "It's time for the school bus. So we'll wait until after school to settle this. I'm going to put Juanita on trial for attempted murder. There are questions and answers that need to be addressed before we can determine who is guilty and who is innocent." With that, Claudene and I went to school. But by the time we reached school, everyone knew I was accused of attempted murder!

School was tough that day, not that anyone bothered me. Most of the children acted as if nothing had happened. And, of course, this left me time to wonder about the trial. What would happen? Whatever it was, I was glad. Claudene was a tyrant and I was tired of having to go to war for myself and my younger sisters, not to mention the two little black girls who were our playmates.[4]

Quite some time before this, my younger sister Sarah, Mousie, Alice and I were playing jump-rope. All of a sudden, Claudene came and took away our rope. Then she proceeded to beat us until we fell on the ground crying. With my face in the dirt, wet with tears, I saw her throw down the rope and walk away, telling us, "That should teach you." As she left, I watched her fat legs, becoming suddenly angry! I snatched up the rope and slung it in such a way it wrapped around both her legs. Then I yanked the rope, snatching her down. With the free end I began whipping her until she begged, "Please War,

---

[4]   Mousie and Alice.

stop beating me! Please War, stop! I heard about four "Please Wars" before I finally let up. I also got her to agree she'd never do this again. Where mother and Isabella were all this time I never did find out, but thank goodness they were not around or I wouldn't have had my way!

Claudene, true to her promise, never interfered with our games again. But she had other ways of tormenting me and one of those ways was wearing my new dresses. And her doing so that particular morning when I pulled the chair out was by no means the first time.

The jump rope incident ran through my mind as the school bus brought us home from school. It was now almost supper time. But supper would be delayed because Uncle Clarence met us at the bus-stop and immediately escorted us to a large room that had been set up for court. As my sister and I entered the room, I looked around. Everybody on the farm was there. Nobody smiled and nobody greeted me, and when I saw my Grandpa Bill dressed like the preacher he was, I no longer wondered at my fate. I was done for!

Uncle Clarence began to address the room full of people. He began by saying he was trying to decide who, among us, he would choose as judge, someone who could be fair. I don't remember anything about a jury being appointed, perhaps because I was already presumed guilty. They just had to decide what to do with me afterward and that's where the judge came in.

While this was going on, I began to pray: "Please God, don't let grandpa be my judge, he will punish me for sure!" All the while, no one said anything and it was sure becoming scary!

Uncle Clarence cut an imposing figure as he looked out over the audience. He cleared his throat and made a very wise decision. He insisted we appoint Allen, Sugar's husband, to act as judge. Allen was a huge black man who had little to say to most people. But he was always kind, polite and adored his little wife. I later learned they were unable to have children of their own. Perhaps for that reason Allen never played with any of the children on the farm and he seemed stern with us. But he was nevertheless always helpful and kind.

My lawyer made plans for me and Judge Allen was a part of that. The judge took a soup ladle and rapped it on a makeshift lectern my uncle found somewhere. Everyone became silent. Looking from face to face, I could pretty well count myself out.

My lawyer stood up and addressed the judge. "Sir, I would like to call my first witness." With the judge's permission, my uncle then called the witness. "Will Claudene Winters please come and stand before the judge."

Claudene's eyes flew wide open and mother and Isabella both started to go up with her. But Uncle Clarence stopped them. "Just Claudene, please."

"Now Claudene," he said, "stand here before Judge Allen and tell him what happened this morning." Claudene came before the judge with downcast eyes and said, "I don't know."

"Are you saying nothing happened Claudene?" asked my uncle. Prompted this way, Claudene blurted out, "Juanita snatched my chair from under me. She made me fall and hurt myself!"

"Why would she do this to you?" my uncle asked.

Claudene lowered her big eyes and pouted her lips as she said in little more than a whisper, "I don't know."

"What did you do to her, Claudene?" asked Uncle Clarence. My mother was getting furious and I knew my lawyer was going to get it when this was over, if not before. And I knew he knew it too. But he continued until Claudene confessed to wearing my new dress without permission. To top it all she sweetened the pot by adding, "But I always wear her dresses whenever I want to!"

I suppose she volunteered this information thinking it would help. But that was all Uncle Clarence needed. He turned to Judge Allen and said, "Your honor, I rest my case."

About this time, father came into the room and sat down

beside mother. I never knew if he had just gotten home or whether he had delayed coming in. When daddy was seated, Judge Allen rose and looked out over the audience.

"To begin," he said in a clear, strong voice, "we should all feel a measure of guilt here." As he cast his steady gaze around the room he continued, "Because we are all guilty. We have quite a few children on this farm and they all play together – except Claudene." Judge Allen looked from one person to the other and continued. "This was not Claudene's fault. It was her mother's fault with the help of Isabella. Beginning tomorrow, I insist on seeing Claudene play with the other children. Her mother and Isabella must stay away from the playground. I am going to appoint Sugar the children's constant companion and disciplinarian. She, in turn, will ask for the mother's help only if needed... Isabella will be given the responsibility of nursing Granny. She is a good nurse."

Judge Allen sat down. Uncle Clarence then announced, "Court is adjourned." "Thank the Lord!" I said.

It wasn't long before I became aware how wise my lawyer and judge really were. I was no longer an angry little girl and the trial taught me how the force of anger, uncontrolled, can destroy.

Claudene also learned from the trial. Well, sorta. As she famously quipped later, "I really like playing with everyone and won't have to wear anymore of Juanita's dresses!"

Ho, boy!!

AUNT MIN AND THE
ANGEL UNAWARE

One warm morning in June, Sugar and several older children, including me, went to pick blackberries at the blackberry patch near our farmhouse. We had to be careful near the bushes and trees, however, because the rattlesnakes were there, laying in the shade waiting for birds. Like us, the birds were after the berries and the rattlesnakes were after the birds. Sometimes, a snake would become excited and try to get one of us if we got too careless. But fortunately, I never knew of a single child that got bit for being that careless.

In no time we picked huge baskets of berries and scampered home. The day was hot and we were thirsty, so we ran to the farmhouse in search of a cool drink. As we did, the most beautiful soprano voice rose to greet us. We had never heard such singing before. It was so beautiful we stopped to listen. The sound appeared to be coming from the farmhouse, so we again ran in that direction, dumbfounded by what we heard. When we arrived, we were startled to see Aunt Min standing in the kitchen, tears spilling down her face. At the window stood Angel, gazing far away. She was singing!

To begin, I want to say that for each of us, both white and black, Angel was someone special. It is true she was different from the rest of us. I would look into other homes to see if they had someone like her. Then I would think "Well, they should have. Every home needs an Angel!"

Angel was about sixteen, short in height and stocky built. She had beautiful long black hair and the white, white skin that is typical of many people in Georgia. She also had the slanting eyes of Down's syndrome.

She seemed to have two brains as well. One to figure out the most uncanny thoughts; the other in which to store all our names. She could always call us by name if she needed to, for she knew she belonged to each of us, anywhere on the farm. She also had the sweetest disposition, that is, until someone tried to order her around.

So here we were, in the kitchen, listening to her sing. It was amazing. The room soon filled with everyone within the sound of her voice. When the song ended, Angel looked at no one in particular but simply walked outside to the barnyard. We who were left behind looked at each other in amazement. This was the first time anything like this had ever happened and we wondered if it would ever happen again.

Like Angel, Aunt Min was also very different. She was a tiny lady, a neighbor who had a large farm and drove a six passenger surrey. Although daddy said she needed four horses, she always hitched just two. As far as I knew, she wasn't kin to anybody, yet she counted in the lives of all of us, and even beyond throughout the whole state of Georgia.

She could do anything. She could help you build a barn or preach a sermon. I don't think she ever had a husband and didn't look as if she needed one.

She was well informed politically and when our Governor, Gene Talmadge, came to South Georgia, he would always invite

29

Aunt Min to go with him to reach the people. Because of this, I don't believe anybody in South Georgia ever voted for anyone but Gene Talmadge.[5]

Aunt Min was a very bright lady. But she had some hang-ups, as we would say today. For one thing, she never washed her hair. Because of this, it was always black as smut and slick as oilcloth. If anyone ever said anything to her about it, Aunt Min would simply reply, "If you be all the time washing your hair, it'll turn gray and fall out."

I think Aunt Min was Irish - Black Irish, it was said. She was also a member of some political group. A hard worker and pillar of society, she knew many things we did not. For instance, we had never seen nor heard of a Down's syndrome child. We knew Angel was different but didn't know why.

When Angel came into the world, Aunt Min would visit often and teach her many things. One day, when she was holding the child, who had not yet been named, she remarked, "She's an angel unaware." After that, we called her "Angel."

After we discovered she could sing, we naturally tried to coax her to sing every so often, but she only just looked at us. Try as we might, we never could persuade her. She acted as if we had a secret we weren't sharing with her. So she denied us her great talent.

Most of the families on our farm had to use the fingers of both hands to count their children. Each of the black families had several and our family had acquired a set of twin girls. Allen and Sugar, my favorite people, still did not have any, however.[6] I think perhaps after Allen served as Judge at my

---

[5] Gene Talmadge (1884 – 1946) campaigned as a dirt farmer without any book learning, but in fact had a law degree from the University of Georgia. He became Georgia's 67th governor in 1933.

[6] As the reader is aware, Allen was married to Isabella, so the meaning is he and his wife did not have children, nor did Sugar and her husband.

trial it softened him, and he was at least more willing to take our farm children under his care.[7]

For instance, early one morning he came to gather us children to take us to our playhouse. I remember how excited I was and the fun I anticipated. However, the thought did cross my mind that I was getting too big for this. In my mind's eye, I never got too old for anything, just too big. This is still true today. As the years have passed, I have grown smaller again. So life is still so much fun for me. I will never get too big nor too old for a fun day!

Anyhow, just as we reached the playhouse area, we spied Aunt Min coming in her surrey. She had the big buggy loaded with a large table and a dozen little straight chairs "Uncle" Allen had made for our playhouse.

The playhouse was built on a hard, flat area located in the Hickory-nut orchard. This was a cool place to play and usually very safe. We got the playhouse cleaned by sweeping with a gall berry broom, then laid out the table and chairs. After this, we all climbed into the surrey and rode back to the farmhouse. There we got all the cold biscuits we could find plus our little tin plates. We also stole a bag of sugar.

Angel was also getting kinda big for this playhouse picnic but she and Aunt Min were coming too. They planned to help pick the berries for our pies. And they also brought the spoons we needed. Boy, were we having a good time!!! When the berries were picked and divided among us children, we each found a seat at the playhouse table, sitting in our new chairs.

Everyone was busily making their pie by splitting a cold biscuit on their plate, then pouring berries on the biscuits and sprinkling them with a handful of sugar.

Suddenly, Angel stopped making her pie. She also stopped laughing or talking and instead cast her eyes down

---

[7] See "On Trial For Attempted Murder at Age Seven."

on her lap. She acted as if she wanted to be someplace else. Everyone became quiet and as Angel raised her eyes to look beyond the seated children, a black and white streak flashed across the front of the table, about three feet away. The bushes near the end of the table became a battleground! We now saw that the black and white flash had become a writhing, twisting king snake! There was also an object of many colors writhing and twisting with him. We children were too terrified to move.

The battle lasted only a few seconds. Soon, the king snake quietly slid away, leaving a huge rattlesnake with a broken neck, behind. I now understood why grandpa always told us, "Never kill a king snake. He is a friend to man."

Though it appeared we were safe, Aunt Min nevertheless got us into the surrey and took us home. We knew we had just had an unforgettable experience.

The following Sunday as we were leaving for church, grandma told us, "Don't forget to thank the lord for the king snake." We promised to do so, everyone except Angel. All the way to church and even once we arrived, she maintained an odd silence. But once the pastor announced that we were to sing "Amazing Grace," before anyone else could begin, Angel stood up and sang the song in its entirety. Those who had not heard her sing before, and even those of us who had, were amazed and enraptured by her beautiful voice. It was as if an angel had come and took possession of her body. The extraordinary vision and sound made us feel we were witnessing a miracle!

The mysteries of the Down's syndrome child are many and sometimes story-like. When Angel stood up to sing, one would think she had been handed a script. The words came without hesitation, as did the notes of her voice. And I have wondered many times throughout the years: could the wonderful work being done today for the Down's syndrome child have brought to the surface the great talent Angel had? Or was it something in the unique training Aunt Min had given her when she was growing up?

I only heard Angel sing twice in her long life. Personally, I have always thought God gives each of us something special to store in our memory bank. For Angel, the words to "Amazing Grace" will forever be the most special to me.

COUSIN ELLICK AND LITTLE SARAH

I recall as a young child living in a large farm community. All the people living in this community were kinfolk. You never referred to any of these people by their first names without a pre-fix indicating what kin they were. For instance, if you had a great-great grandmother named Mary, she was known as "Grandma Mary." So it was with aunts, uncles or cousins. Cousins would sometimes marry if they were far enough removed. But judging by the outcome, some of us were probably not removed far enough!

Cousin Ellick was a special cousin we liked and were proud of having in the family. A third cousin to my father (and about his age), he was far enough removed we weren't constantly having to make excuses for his peculiar habits. He was very wealthy and lived a quite dignified lifestyle with his mother. And they had a large black woman named "Lizzer" who lived in their home and looked after them. Lizzer commanded respect and ran the household. She had a good heart, too. For instance, she always had a buttered biscuit for any child who came around.

As for Cousin Ellick, rumor had it he bought a car. And sure enough, one day he drove up - or rather his driver drove him up – to our home. It caused quite a commotion and we all ran out to greet him. At that time there might have been a few Model T trucks around, but I believe he was the first person in our area to own a car. We were still rather proud of our horse and buggy carriages and had not considered a car an improvement. Nevertheless, Cousin Ellick became something of a spectacle now that he had one.

It was a Nash, a big monster of a thing that could easily cause a nightmare if you met it on the road. During that time the first cars and the many horse and buggies were not too happy together.

As I mentioned, Cousin Ellick's arrival in his new car created quite a stir. All the more when we learned Cousin Ellick had come to take little Sarah for a ride. Little Sarah was about thirteen years of age, just a year younger than me, a beautiful girl with bright auburn hair and huge blue eyes. People who saw her would readily think of a little angel except for the bountiful red curls on her head.

Frankly, we all knew little Sarah was a handful. And the fact Cousin Ellick made a remark that was none too kind to my older sister and me made us look forward to what he was in for. When asked why he chose Little Sarah to court instead of us, he said "Because you're too old!" He further commented on the fact we were "… dating boys!" I was only fourteen and Claudene barely fifteen at the time. So there! Claudene and I had good reason to make life topsy-turvy for Cousin Ellick. And Little Sarah was always ready to join in with our plans. As for Claudene, despite the problems we had had earlier in our lives, we had finally learned to get along if it benefited us to do so. So we whispered to Little Sarah that we wanted her to make Cousin Ellick take us along for the ride too. Immediately she turned her big eyes and sweet smile on Cousin Ellick. "I will go for a ride with you if Claudene and Juanita can go also."

He didn't like it but was just about to settle us all in the car when daddy came running out. He told Cousin Ellick we couldn't go because we had to get back to the cotton patch with everyone else on the place. It was true. Everybody on our farm, black and white, picked cotton. By now, Cousin Ellick was getting frustrated. "I will pay somebody to pick cotton for Little Sarah," he nearly shouted. Then he added, "When she marries me, she won't have to pick cotton!" That did it, I thought. Cousin Ellick's done for! Sure enough, daddy ran at Cousin Ellick, Cousin Ellick ran for the car, and his driver took off to the woods! When Cousin Ellick saw that his driver had left him, he jumped in the car, jammed it in forward and sped away barely missing trees, people, and dogs! He finally got the car turned toward home, going from ditch to ditch on either side of the road until he was soon out of sight.

It was a shocking state of affairs! But after a few minutes, we all burst out laughing. It was at this point father decided he had better go see if Cousin Ellick got home alright. After all, crazy or not, Cousin Ellick was still his cousin.

When daddy reached Cousin Ellick's home, he found the ol' fellow sitting in the car inside his barn. He had built a shed to house the car several weeks earlier. So into this shed he had driven his car, close against the inside wall, with only a few nicks and scratches. Meanwhile, the horses who lived in the barn were lined up against the opposite wall. They all knew they had been invaded but they didn't know by what.

Daddy first calmed the horses, then got Cousin Ellick out of the car and into the care of Lizzer. As for the car, it was never driven again. Cousin Ellick became a recluse and lived in his home another thirty years before his sister decided it was time for him to break up housekeeping. He was getting too old to stay alone. Lizzer and his mother had passed away long before.

When the farm was sold, the car was still there, sitting right where Cousin Ellick had parked it all those years before. It must have been sold or given away, but I'm not really sure.

I do know Little Sarah never rode in the car and Cousin Ellick never came to call on her again. It was sad in a way, especially what became of Cousin Ellick, but the love of an older man for such a young girl, and a cousin to boot, was doomed from the start. Perhaps it is different today, but the outcome was not uncommon for a period seventy-five years ago, or thereabouts.

I was reading in our family history book the other day where several male ancestors had two or three wives and reared up to twenty-five children in some cases. Life at that time was hard for women. Nevertheless, I recall most of my ancestors living in beautiful homes and having plenty of servants which allowed them to maintain a comfortable lifestyle. The men in the family usually had two or three wives not from divorce, for this was rare, but because the wife usually did not live long after giving birth to so many children. The man then married another young girl and she began having too many children, and the best of care for young mothers was not all that good a century ago.

As I read the family history, I naturally thought of Little Sarah. She is still living and has outlived two husbands.[8] Unlike many women of the period, she was a survivor. Her red hair and striving for independence made a fighter out of her. In fact, we have had some good times reminiscing our younger years.

---

[8]   Sadly, Little Sarah would pass away during the writing of these stories.

THE DANCING GHOSTS

Speaking with Little Sarah the other day, she asked if I remembered the plantation house our Granda Bill built in the late eighteen eighties.[9] I did indeed! "I have been searching for someone who knows when the old plantation house was torn down," I told her.

Haskel Edmondson, a cousin who lives in Barney, had the information I needed. The mansion had not been torn down but instead sold to three different families. If grandpa could look down on things, I'm sure he'd be happy. For just as he once took pride seeing his eight sons grow up in this home, I know he would want to see these several families prosper.

Little Sarah also asked if I remembered grandpa's house being haunted. I remembered this, too. For after he passed away the home became vacant, and stories began circulating that anyone passing the house after midnight would see lights come on, hear music play and see beautiful ladies and handsomely dressed men dancing in the upstairs ballroom! Personally, I found it curious there were people who could tell this story but never its ending. I suppose this is because most

---

[9] According to Dr. Stephen W. Edmondson, family historian, the house was built approximately 1891 and demolished in 1991. It was situated a few hundred yards west of what is now Georgia Highway 76, just south of Morven. One large, live oak tree still survives along Jones Creek Road where the house once stood.

people in Georgia are afraid of ghosts. They might see them but don't want to stay around to have a conversation! In my entire life I never sought them out but one time. And that was the night some teenagers and I decided to see for ourselves whether the story about grandfather's house was really true.

We were lead in this adventure by my mother's youngest brother, Cousin Epp.[10] Epp swore he had heard the music and seen the dancing several times. He also said the lights came on once the music started.

I was just a country girl who had never seen a house with electric lights. Our house, for example, had no electricity and consequently we still used oil lamps. So actually, I was more interested in seeing how the lights came on, especially in a house that had no electricity, than seeing how ghosts danced.

Anyway, on the particular night Cousin Epp lead us to the haunted house, the moon fought with the flitting clouds but never quite won. So there we were walking along the dark unpaved roads, our hearts beating faster as we got closer.

Seeing the house at night was different from seeing it in the daytime.

Grandpa's house was three stories high with porches on each floor all around. In truth, it looked like a big monster that had just swooped down. To us children, frightened as we already were, the house certainly looked haunted, ghosts or no ghosts!

With the house in view, Epp herded us into the semi-darkness of several large trees across from the house itself. He told us we could see everything that went on upstairs and for us to all stay together on the patch of grass where he had placed us. All in all, there were about twenty-five of us. Most, like myself, were fourteen or fifteen. But a few, like Epp, were

---

[10] According to Ms. Kate Holmes, daughter of cousin Frances, "Cousin Epp" was in fact Enoch Pike (E.P. or "Epp") Edmondson, Juanita's uncle by true relation.

eighteen or older. Epp told us we should sit very still and remain quiet; the dancers would not come if they knew we were watching. You could see big, frightened eyes everywhere. Everyone was scared to death, including Epp.

Because we were sitting on the grass, many of us were even more scared than we might have been. For we knew rattlesnakes liked to sleep in warm places. Had we stayed on the ground, we might have had a lap full of rattlesnake! Soon, however, somebody brought benches. Who these people were, or where they got the benches, we had no idea. All we knew was that we were off the grass and could worry about ghosts rather than snakes.

So here we were on the benches high as a kite due to fear and anticipation. We wanted to see the dancing ghosts but were nevertheless terrified at the prospect. That is when I found out ghost hunting produces a special aura. It's something that surrounds you, gets in your hair, and the hair and features of everyone around you. I can't explain it really, except that it's physical, and also psychological.

As we waited, Epp instructed us to watch the ballroom window on the upper floor. Consequently, all of us had our eyes riveted on this part of the house. Suddenly, Junior, a favorite cousin of mine who was sitting directly behind me, pulled my hair. I screamed, then whirled around and slapped him. Just as I did, the first light in the ballroom appeared. Then came the music. And a sound like a groan or maybe an exclamation was heard from everyone who watched. But before anyone could recover, another light appeared, then another and still another.

We kept watching as the upper story of the house gradually became illuminated. At first there was nothing but the lights and music, but soon beautifully dressed people came into view and we actually saw they were dancing!

So there really were dancing ghosts!!!

At that moment, all of us seemed frozen in time, every eye glued to the lighted ballroom. And I'm sure the spell would have captivated us a very long while had not my cousin Frances jumped up screaming, trying to run away. Obviously the experience was too much for her. Of course it had always been my impression Frances lived in a land of make-believe; the very idea she could out-run a ghost was ridiculous! But no matter how silly, her action was like a spark in a tinderbox. Epp tried to save the situation by running after her. But before he had gone very far, everyone, including myself, was running and screaming, several of us colliding in the darkness.

Only now it wasn't as dark anymore. The lights in the ballroom were descending! Looking over my shoulder, I saw the dancing ghosts were no longer in the ballroom but appeared to be coming after us! So we all ran faster, screaming till our voices gave out, each of us trying to reach grandfather's house about two miles away. There we knew we would find safety and shelter, for that is where we were supposed to be spending the weekend.

As we reached grandpa's house, I looked around to see there were no lights following us, no beautiful women and no beautifully dressed men. Instead, the girls and boys running from the lights were crying, limping and falling all about. Several had bruised angles and cut feet. When we were counted by the several adults who came outside to learn what had happened, it was found that not a single child had been caught by the ghosts.

Epp, for his part, seemed to be mad at us the rest of the weekend. I'm pretty sure I saw grandpa taking him to the woodshed. And I'm also fairly certain it wasn't to cut wood! Just prior to our adventure, Epp had sworn us to secrecy so our parents and grandparents wouldn't know what we were up to. Now that it was known, he had had to pay the price for being our leader.

Nothing was ever explained about the dancing ghosts. Epp didn't tell, nor did anyone else. I did hear it whispered that several young ladies spent the night in the haunted house about the time we were there. But was this the same night we saw the dancing ghosts? Did the lights run off and leave them and forget to come back?

Epp never talked about that night. And he died with his secret, several years ago. In my life, I have seen several events I could not explain and the dancing ghosts was one of them.

But as I have mentioned somewhere else in this book, I hit the floor running when the Granny Woman delivered me. I suppose I was afraid she might send me back! And I've been on top of things pretty well ever since. So I worked out a theory for the dancing ghosts I think explains the whole thing. Though fairly certain of this explanation, I have never told anyone while Cousin Epp was alive, knowing he wouldn't like it. Now that he's dead, however, I feel I should keep his secret. But if anyone reading this story figures it out, so be it.

William A. Edmondson,
1847-1930, aka "Grandpa Bill"

Sophronia Hendry Edmondson,
1850-1906, wife of William A.

The William Edmondson Family, as taken by a
traveling photographer in 1892. Seated, left to right:
William Edmondson, Sophronia Edmondson,
and Sophronia's father, the Reverend John M.
Hendry. Behind is the home mentioned in
"The Dancing Ghosts."

Enoch Pike Edmondson, aka "Ol' Man Oss"
(1869-1942) and his wife Emma Elmira Simpson
(1873-1941). The E.P. Edmondsons were
Hazel Juanita's maternal grandparents.

Enoch Pike Edmondson's children,
1906. Included is Hazel Juanita's mother,
Ruth, age 10, second from the left.

Clarence Luther Edmondson (1881-1953),
son of William A., the budding attorney
who defended Hazel Juanita in "On Trial for
Attempted Murder at the Age of Seven."

Willis Flournoy Edmondson (1879-1966),
son of William A., who was both a scholar
and ran the dry goods store mentioned
in "Mousie's Getting Married."

Cornelia May Edmondson (1898-1986), daughter of James William Edmondson (1874-1900) and granddaughter of William A. As an only child, she was reared in Grandfather Edmondson's home. Photo taken circa 1914 at a time when she was "sweet sixteen."

A BUNCH OF CRAZZIES!

Uncle Gus and Aunt Mary, two of our beloved older black people, died within a few days of each other. Their deaths, so close together, put a strain on the ol' cooling board. But everyone worked around the clock to get the two old bodies straight and tall for their journey into heaven.

I think I was about fourteen at the time. I had a beautiful red handkerchief Aunt Mary always admired. So I asked permission to place the handkerchief in her hand. And I remember thinking: why didn't I give it to her sooner?

Anyway, after the wake and burial, mother and father had to decide what to do with Gus and Mary's empty house down near the creek.

The old couple had long gotten too old to do much work. But they continued living in the little creek house just the same. And when we went down to enjoy ourselves in the cool creek water, Aunt Mary would always bring us some of her homemade cookies to snack on while we were playing.

The old house was empty now, sadly reminding us Uncle Gus and Aunt Mary were gone. Never more would we enjoy their company nor the cookies they brought us down by the creek. And always when passing the creek house thereafter, or the gently flowing waters nearby, we recalled our many pleasant memories of these people and how it had been when they were alive.

But despite our sad remembrance, we still roamed this part of the farm. Mousie and Alice, almost marrying age now, along with Sarah, Margie and I, were everywhere all day long when we didn't have cotton to pick. Sarah and Margie were my two younger sisters. Together, we weren't afraid of anything, even rattlesnakes.

One hot morning, we ran down to play in the water behind the creek house. But we were stopped in our tracks by a strange sight. There on the creek house porch, three half-naked white boys about our age were stretched out sleeping. Without a word, we whirled around and ran back to the house. We were told by Isabella, the black woman who took care of our kitchen, that a white family had moved into the creek house. You could tell Isabella didn't like it and neither did we.

What were they doing there? Were they going to make moonshine for father? Everyone knew our black folks made the best liquor in Georgia. So why would daddy hire a white family to do this – unless it was for something else? What could it be?

At first, I think we felt a measure of privacy invasion. We had never been allowed to play with share-croppers' children, for they were considered "poor white trash." I thought this stupid at the time, and still do. Although we picked cotton along with our blacks, most poor white folks didn't have to. Despite being "poor white trash," they were the lucky ones.

Anyway, we didn't know what these white folks were doing in the little creek house, but we did learn this at supper that night. Their name was "Bruce" and they had three boys and a girl who was a few years older. We also learned Mr. Bruce was going to train and take care of the livestock. Our livestock consisted of horses, mules, cows, and other animals. We children seldom had trouble catching any animal we wanted to ride unless it was a Billy goat or a bull cow in love. Sometimes we got jarred around a bit, so maybe this Mr. Bruce would improve the situation.

It was several months before we would learn these people

were from New York City. This fact was not a recommendation as far as we were concerned. To work on a farm in South Georgia required an appreciation for the country. Not only this, it required good, common horse sense! The Bruce's, we figured, didn't have this. But they did have spunk and soon we would realize just how much fun we would have watching them handle our farm animals!

For instance, Ben, their smallest boy, wanted to ride the Shetland pony. The pony was small so Ben thought he could handle him pretty easily. Ben approached the pony, threw his leg across and sat up straight, holding the bridle somebody placed in the pony's mouth. For a moment, everything was fine and the little boy had a smile on his face.

The next moment, the pony's hind end shot in the air, he lowered his head and Ben shot plum over, hitting the ground head first. The pony took off and Ben just laid where he'd landed. "Woewee!," I shrieked, "This situation's looking up! We might have some excitement with this bunch of crazies!"

Aside from Ben, there was Bo and Boaz. The two older boys looked alike except one had black hair and the other red hair. Other than this, they were about the same size.

Mr. "red hair" (Bo) strolled over to Ben who was still lying on the ground. The Shetland pony was already eating grass several yards away.

Bo, who was the elder of the group, pulled Ben up and stood him on his feet. Little Ben was kinda shaky and had dirt and blood all over his head and face. Bo and Boaz were laughing at him. Boaz, undaunted by Ben's failure, declared he could ride that "little ol' horse." We girls knew he couldn't ride that "little ol' horse," for it was the meanest animal on the farm!

All the Shetland ponies I've ever seen were temperamental at best and most of the time they could throw you off no matter how you were trying to ride them. And if you somehow manage to hold on to one, he would suddenly stop and grab your clothes (hopefully your clothes and not your leg) and pull you off his back. By this time, you were so frightened you hit the ground running, desperately trying to avoid his kicking feet.

Boaz strolled over to within ten feet of the Shetland, who was grazing on the grass. All of us except Bo, Ben and Boaz, knew the pony was watching every move he made. The boys thought the pony had forgotten them. So while the pony continued eating, Boaz quietly crept up on his backside. Suddenly, he jumped on the pony, straddling him and grabbing him around the neck. The pony kicked up his hind legs, lowered his head, screamed like a wild cat, then took off running!

Boaz was never so scared in his life! He was scared to hold on and just as scared to turn loose. The "little horse" kicked up his heels, lowered his head and did all his usual tricks. But Boaz, frozen with terror, was hugging the Shetland with all his might.

Suddenly, the pony stopped and threw himself on the ground, rolling over and over, rolling Boaz with him. Boaz let out a scream, then a few howls, whereupon the "little horse" jumped up and ran away. Soon, the horse was on a high grassy knoll eating grass watching those of us who remained below.

Daddy and Mr. Bruce went to help Boaz. He was somewhat disoriented and seemed to be in shock. On examination, they found he had a broken leg somewhere near the ankle. And the big toe on the other foot was pointing to the sky.

Since Boaz wasn't one of his young'uns, daddy decided he might better take him to the new hospital in Quitman to have him fixed up. I remember thinking if I had a broken leg, our Granny Woman would have fixed it. "Oh, well," I thought. "I'm not going to break my leg because I have sense enough not to ride that Shetland pony!" There's an old saw that says there has to be some love between a Shetland pony and its owner. For only the owner can ride him.

As predicted, the Bruce boys never rode the "little ol' horse." But as time went on, we watched those New York City boys try different things and fall on their faces, only to get up and try to tackle something else. The black children on the farm watched the boys as we did, and their eyes just got bigger and bigger.

These boys were funny to me by the way they clipped their words and left half the word in their mouth. But it was also funny to see them stand on their heads to watch the pigs eat slop. I soon realized the problem wasn't that they weren't bright, they were just ignorant. For instance, one hot summer day, I went to the woods with the women and children, both black and white, to pick berries. We kept hearing something that sounded like a young calf calling his mamma. This sound followed us as we left the berry patch, but no one could see anything. We were all getting frightened and began hurrying faster and faster. But the noise of the baby calf seemed to stay with us.

When we reached home we ran into the kitchen and told Isabella something was following us. Isabella opened the door and when she did, Bo dashed in carrying an armful of brown fur. While we were picking berries, Bo had caught a little brown bear and had now brought it home with him!

"He was picking berries and eating them, so I thought he was hungry and brought him home. I wanted to give him some food!" The story went around the farm and even the community. And this is when the expression "a bunch of crazies" was first used.

All our black men thought Bo was the dumbest boy they had ever seen. "To catch a bear and fetch him home was not only dumb, it was dangerous," they said. The mamma bear would surely have killed Bo if she had caught him. The truth is, Bo didn't know what he had caught, let alone a bear. This is why I defended Bo by telling everyone he was merely ignorant. As for Bo, he was a happy boy and didn't seem to worry one way or the other about his mental status.

Meanwhile, daddy was trying to figure out a way for Bo to keep the bear. Bo was so tickled over the animal, daddy thought maybe he could find a way. But he knew if he put it in a cage, the mamma bear would come and get him, cage and all!

Bo was against the idea of a cage too. He said he would rather let the bear sleep with him! So right then and there daddy decided Bo wasn't just ignorant, he was dumb! The little creek house wasn't strong enough to withstand a large brown bear looking for its baby. I think daddy finally convinced Bo it would be better to let the little brown bear sleep in a large cardboard box near the creek bed.

So Bo enjoyed feeding the little bear and taking care of him until bedtime. Then the bear was put in the large cardboard box and Bo and Bo's parents were instructed to stay away from the box until the sun came up the next morning.

But daddy didn't trust the Bruce's. He felt their lack of knowledge about bears might prove dangerous and he didn't want to wake up the next morning and find the results of a mamma bear having rescued her young one.

So he appointed two of our most trustworthy black men to keep watch until the mamma bear came for her baby. The next morning they reported the mamma bear came, gave the baby bear a good grooming (to take away the scent of man) and left with it in tow, as quietly as she had come. And it seemed that she had no fear of man, for she came while the houses on the farm were still lighted. Since the time I was a small child, I have watched how each animal knows its purpose in the world and acts accordingly. Only man seems to behave differently.

Boaz stayed in the hospital a couple of weeks, but when he came home, was still limping rather badly. That's when I noticed my sister Sarah taking over his care more and more, a situation which didn't please mother.

Mrs. Bruce and her daughter Adell never came away from the creek house. I suppose they sensed mamma was not interested in knowing them. Mamma, more than likely, thought they weren't our class of people and let them know this one way or the other.

Just as many of us, black and white, began to feel the Bruce family was becoming a part of the farm, Mr. Bruce decided to pull up stakes and take his family back to New York City. I'm sure his wife and daughter were glad to leave, for they probably thought it was we who were crazy. I don't think they ever understood a thing we said. And I know we never understood their language. After all, they were full-blooded Yankees!!

Bo, Ben and Boaz seemed sad to leave. And even though Boaz was still limping when they left, he went and found the "little ol' horse" and waved goodbye - from a distance! As for Bo, I think he was looking forward to catching another brown bear, if only he could hide him from his mother... Ho-boy!

As the years went by and we didn't hear from the Bruce's anymore, I wondered what became of them and whether Boaz got to walking better and Bo collected any more pets. I'm sure their being on our farm taught them something, even if it took going back to the big city to find out what it was.

WHITE-LIGHTNING
MADNESS

Fall was in the air! The potatoes had been dug and the cotton had all been picked and sold. Cotton was about the only money crop we South Georgia folks grew. Most of the other crops – potatoes, for instance - were for feeding the families that lived on our farm. We considered ourselves blessed if we had a good growing season, for that meant we would have plenty of food to see us through winter.

I don't recall there ever being any real worry on the part of the adults on our farm. For in addition to the harvest, the rivers and lakes always provided plenty of fish, ducks and other game - even rattlesnake. Most of us knew how delicious fried rattlesnake could be a long time before it became a popular delicacy. Nowadays, of course, there are huge rattlesnake round-ups, where not only the meat is served, but venom is collected to make antidote. Antidote, too, existed long before the round-ups, and daddy carried a snake bite kit with him everywhere and at all times once they were available.

I remember one particular occasion when he needed it. It was a day when all the men were pulling corn to be stored for winter and also for making white-lightning. The day was hot and the tall corn stalks made it rather difficult and unpleasant for the workers.

When they could, the men would sometimes climb upon a rail fence to catch a cool breath of air and rest a while. They would also drink plenty of water. So on this particular occasion, the men were sitting on a fence looking out over the corn field waiting for the water boy to bring a bucket of water.

Suddenly, one of the men sitting on the fence began climbing down. It was a young black man who had been visiting his grandmother almost all summer. He did not live on our place but his grandmother did for as long as I can remember. He came to stay with her and worked on the farm to earn some money. He was a good farm worker and daddy was hoping he would stay.

But when the young man began climbing down from the fence, the other men began to murmur, "He's had it! He's quitting!" Indeed, the boy seemed to be in a daze, as if he'd been in the sun too long.

But as he got off the fence, he walked straight ahead, reached down and picked up a huge rattlesnake! He was holding the wiggling, writhing snake, gripping it just behind the jaws. The snake's mouth was open and the boy seemed to be in a trance. All the men on the fence yelled at him to "throw the snake down!" They realized the young man had been charmed. It was common knowledge going back a hundred years or so that rattlesnakes charmed birds, and some felt they could also charm humans. Personally, I don't know that I believe this. I do know you loose the power to move if you suddenly walk up on one. But truly I think the rattler just scares you to death. The charm part's for the birds.

Getting back to our story, however, with all his co-workers shouting at him, the boy finally realized he was holding a rattler and tried to throw it down. But the snake bit the young man on the forearm as he threw it.

All the men scampered down from the fence to help the snake bitten victim. Some of them grabbed the young man, while another wielded his knife, ready to cut his arm where the snake's fangs went in. This was a common method for saving someone's life when they were snake bit. Someone would slash the area and proceed to suck the venom out. But this wasn't sure-fire. Sometimes the snake bitten person and the person sucking the venom both died!

About this time, however, hearing the commotion, daddy came running, hollering, "Don't cut him! I've got a new snake bite kit. Let's give it a try."

To be sure, some of the first snake bite kits were not always successful. But this one worked and except for a badly swollen arm, the young man got better in just a few days – not as good as new perhaps - but well on the way to recovery. And I think he rather enjoyed not having to pull corn again; which brings me to our story.

This process of harvesting corn from the fields after it had been allowed to dry was part of the white lightning process. Corn was used in making the white lightning. And the corn had to be thoroughly dry and properly shelled for it to ferment and distill properly.

The kernels used in making white lightning had to be perfect, with no black spots or rot from too much rain. Otherwise, the corn would be sour. As I've said, the kernels had to be perfect.

"Why?" I asked Isabella.

Isabella said the white lightning would kill you if you put bad grain into it. To tell the truth, I saw some mighty sick black folks when they got drunk on the stuff. I don't recall anyone ever dying, however. So if Isabella was right, people getting sick rather than dying owed a debt of gratitude to "perfect" corn.

Now in fact, white lightning is a beautiful, crystal clear liquid like the clearest water you have ever seen. I've heard the men on our farm say when you swallowed it, it felt like fire going down. And when it reached the stomach, you thought a mule had kicked your insides.

Daddy allowed the men on the place to make their own. Most of the time, they grouped together, about three to a group, and each had their own little "still" as it was called, down by the creek. Everybody worked getting the corn, water and sugar measured out and fired up in the still apparatus. Most of the time, syrup was used instead of sugar because we made our own, whereas the sugar had to be purchased.

I don't know the exact process for making white lightning, but I do know a lot of time goes into it, several weeks' worth, and a good part of this involves building and stoking fires. And though I never saw the fires, I was sure this was true, because there'd always be lots of smoke coming from the creek area.

As the year progressed, the weather turned cooler, which meant hog-killing time was getting near. We grew porkers to furnish bacon and ham, and cows for beef. This was the time consuming part of farming but a necessary part, too. Everybody on the farm helped with this operation and were usually happy, for they stayed busy while working together. And we certainly enjoyed the fresh meats afterward, which was a rarity in the summer months. We couldn't afford to buy steak, that's for sure.

Anyway, the hog-killing time usually coincided with the distilling part of the white lightning process, so the latter could be left to itself to turn out as it should. Once all the meat processing work was completed, however, the men were again free to check their liquor. They did this by filling clear glass jars direct from the stills. On one occasion, I remember daddy teasing the men that the liquid they were draining was the "prettiest" clear liquor they had ever made. Teasing or not, the men seemed pleased, and took this as a high compliment.

I should point out that the white lightning was not made to sell. It was made purely to drink, and also for medicine. And one of the rules of the farm was, nobody drank white lightning except on Saturday night, that is, unless he was sick with a cold or flu or some other life-threatening ailment. As I look back, it seemed our farm people sure got sick a lot during the early winter months. But by Christmas, everyone's health had greatly improved. Daddy insisted they keep enough white lightning to celebrate Christmas and they usually did.

Another practice worth mentioning was the feeding of wild turkeys. We usually began doing this around October. The idea was to persuade the birds to stay on the farm so everyone would have a nice, plump turkey for Thanksgiving. Later I would learn feeding wild turkeys was called "bating" and was against the law. But at the time, I don't think we knew this. Instead, we only knew the farmer's first law - the law of survival.

One particular Thanksgiving I'll never forget. And it puts the cap on my story about white lightning. Actually, it was a few nights before Thanksgiving, on an evening when everything was quiet. The moon was bright and there was a chill in the air. I remember we were enjoying a warm fire in the fireplace. Grandpa and I were playing checkers. I also remember that as usual, he was winning. Suddenly, a blood-curdling scream came from down near the creek bank. The scream had hardly died when someone was pounding on the door.

It seemed the scream came from where Mousie and Alice lived. But what could it be? Seldom did we have anything to fear from animals in the area. Sometimes a panther or wild cat might be spotted but not in a populated area. And there was little fear of brown bears, either. The brown bear was perfectly gentle unless a female's baby was in danger.

Daddy already had his gun in hand and I followed behind him. He threw open the door and there stood Duck. Duck looked as if he had just seen something terrible.

"O'mister, O'mister," he said to daddy, looking so pitiful. "Son done kill his Misses!" Daddy took ol' Duck by the arm. "O' maybe not Duck, let's go see."

Now ol' Duck was a character and daddy liked to talk about him because he was amused by his name and how he first showed up at our farm. This huge young man of undetermined origin came walking up one morning as all the men were gathering for work and said to my father, "Mah name iss Duck. I haf uh wife an' three chillun an' wood like ta wurk on diss here farm." Duck looked as if he had Indian and black blood flowing in his veins. Whatever his origins, daddy thought he was a good-looking specimen and so hired him right then and there.

All this was a good while before I was born. By now, Duck had been on our farm a good many years and had reared three little boys into manhood. Yet here he was crying. For it appeared one of his sons had just killed his wife.

Daddy took Duck by the arm and started in the direction of where his son lived. I followed close behind. But as we walked, the old man remembered he had taken his son's wife to his own home for safe keeping. So we went to Duck's home instead. When we got there, the wife was crying and would not come out of the closet. But at least she was alive! After a bit of coaxing, daddy persuaded her to come out and be examined. Looking her over, he found she had a bad gash half way across the top of her head.

Daddy told Duck and me to run and get the Granny Woman. He did not think the wife's skull had been damaged but blood was everywhere and the gash looked none too pretty.

I knew daddy was hoping he could take care of this problem himself. If he could, there would be no need for a doctor. The doctor would make a report and the Sheriff would come looking for Jake, Duck's son. In addition to finding Jake, he might also find the stills. Because of this, the Sheriff made our people nervous and sometimes they would leave.

But it happened the Granny Woman was able to stop the bleeding and sew up the gash in Jake's wife's head. Several of the farm men came to help, so daddy told them to take her to our house in case the husband returned. Daddy knew Jake would never come to our home, so his wife was sure to get a night's rest and recover from her wounds.

Now, it was time to hunt up Jake. This didn't take long. Daddy and the men found him half submerged in the creek near his white lightning still. His head was propped up on a log and the rest of him was in the water. Two empty quart jars lay nearby.

The following day daddy gave the order: "There will be no more white lightning madness on this farm. All of you who make or keep liquor must get rid of it from this day forward!"

Needless to say, Jake was a very unhappy man. But he also had lots of unhappy company.

GRANDPA BILL THE GHOST

While still living, my Grandpa Bill more than once promised, "I will come back, Juanita, if ever you need me. God has promised." He would sometimes say this to me after Sunday services for us children, and once, in particular, when Cousin Myrtle asked him, "Grandpa, what will we do without you when God calls you home?"

Grandpa Bill, a big and tall, kind and gentle man, would look at us with his loving but serious expression, as if he truly believed just what he was saying. But his wife, Grandma Emma, did not like for him to say these things. She wanted us to go directly to God in prayer. Personally, however, I was comforted by what grandpa told us, for I wanted it to be so.

I was 11 years old when grandpa passed away.[11] All the people from miles around attended his funeral. He was dressed in an elegant black suit with his long white beard spread upon his chest. Everyone in the neighborhood and particularly from our farm, both black and white, was saddened by his death. All who attended the funeral passed his casket not once but several times to say "good-bye." We all knew we were going to miss grandpa very much.

---

[11] William Edmondson was born Christmas Day 1847 and died October 27, 1930. He is buried at Mt. Zion Cemetery in Morven, Georgia. "Grandpa Bill" was actually Ms. Collins' great grandfather (mother's side). It was customary, nevertheless, to address him as "grandpa."

Many times after grandpa died, people would stop and recollect on the days when he was still with us. More often than not, this would happen at the big fishpond grandpa had donated to the town, a place where young people went to court or swim. Of course, the older people went there too, for meetings and recreational purposes. And this is where my mother, father, sisters and I would see our neighbors, Sunday afternoons, while strolling the many paths that wound through the woods. Meeting fellow townsfolk and even other relatives, the conversation would often turn to grandfather, his spirit lingering in the tall trees and the smell of Georgia pine. On one of these occasions, there was Aunt Effie's son who said, "Old Man Enoch was a man who stood above the rest." Then there was Mr. Moore, our Superintendent of Schools, who said grandpa was a consistently honest man. Father admitted this too, though he didn't particularly like grandpa, elaborating that he always paid his debts. Grandma Emma, who was born a Simpson, often said the reason she was drawn to grandpa was because he was a good Christian. She said this even though she was a hard-shell Baptist and he was a Methodist preacher. They had had 11 children together. Unfortunately, there had been many other women who had been interested in grandpa, not so much for his Christian beliefs but for his countrified good looks. Not only was he handsome, but friendly and fun-loving.

In fact, the day he died, grandpa was out with another woman. A very young woman. He said his purpose in this - for it was not the first time - was that he wanted the younger people of Morven to enjoy their youth and wanted to see them have a good time. The fact the young people he enjoyed were young women was a matter that today might raise eyebrows. But at the time no one questioned his motives. Even his wife trusted his good intentions and never wavered in this opinion.

On the day in question, a Saturday afternoon, grandpa had invited Mary Bullock to the movie house. As was usual on Saturday, the cinema was full of people.[12] Grandpa took Mary to her seat, but rather than sit next to her, proceeded to gad about and socialize with other people in the audience. Not till the show actually began did he take his place next to Mary. But when he did, the way in which he sat caused the pistol he carried in his back pocket to fire, sending a bullet up through the back of his head, killing him instantly. Naturally, the news of this horrific incident caused a great amount of speculation and sorrow in the community, some wondering why he kept a gun, others suggesting he should have bought one equipped with a trigger-guard and safety.

It is said people who loose their lives through some tragic event are the ones who most often return as spirits to haunt the living. But I do not believe this, rather that grandpa returned because he promised. And besides, the manner of his return was so open and free of any malice as to confirm his good intentions. He was also very prompt. The following is how it occurred.

We were attending church one Sunday, the very day after grandpa was shot. And while we were leaving someone exclaimed, "Say, that's Ol' Man Enoch walking through the cemetery!" Instantly, all the church goers began running towards him. In truth, Grandma Emma claimed she had seen him that morning, but we dismissed the idea on account of her grief. But now, here he was in the churchyard adorned in the dark suite he wore when he preached. So everyone gathered around him, dozens and dozens of people, to gawk and touch him and ask all manner of questions. In gratitude and utter amazement, some began to pray out loud. I, of course, wanted to speak with grandpa too to ask how it was God had granted his vow to return and whether he would come again. But some of the adults, for reasons never explained, began corralling

---

[12] As Morven did not have a movie house, this was the old Ilex theater in Quitman (letter from Dr. Stephen Edmondson to editor, 18 May 2010).

we younger people and leading us away. Perhaps they were worried we'd be frightened. Whatever the reason, neither my sisters nor I ever got a chance to get up close and speak with grandpa. Those who did swore it was him, including some of the most prominent citizens of Morven. But none of them ever spoke much about what they said to him or what he said in return.

Grandpa never returned but that one occasion. His funeral occurred later in the week. I suppose the reason many of the persons who passed his casket did so more than once was because they still weren't convinced he was really dead. To us children, it didn't matter whether grandpa's body lay in the coffin or whether he was buried six feet beneath the hard Georgia clay. We knew his ghost had already appeared and was free to come again. And for many years after, we would joyously remind ourselves how grandpa kept his promise.

THE TREES WALKED
ON WATER

My parents first bought a car when I was ten years old. This was South Georgia in 1929. Money was plentiful and car salesmen were too. So most farmers bought cars but still drove their horse and buggy.

Mamma's little "Mary," a petite red mare that pulled her dashing black buggy, didn't like our new Model A Ford. The Model A was black too, with flapping side curtains.[13] The flapping curtains were no fault of the automobile so much as the fact we didn't fasten them. We knew that if we did, people couldn't see us as we passed by. And we wanted to be seen! The only problem was, when we met a horse and buggy passing on the road, the horse, buggy and people in it usually took off across the field. I'm sure the flapping curtains did it. We were quite a scary sight!

Anyway, mamma seldom drove the Ford. She much preferred little "Mary" and her buggy.

One morning she decided to go fishing. Isabella, a tall pretty black woman who was reared on our farm, always went with her. And on this occasion, I was taken along too.

---

[13] Ford Motor Company manufactured the Model A between the years 1927 and 1932, with a total of some 4,858,000 cars of various body styles. The version Ms. Collins is describing was possibly the Phaeton Deluxe.

Mamma was a good fisherwoman. She never grew tired and always seemed to know just where to throw her line. Her technique was very simple. When she caught a fish she took it off the hook, threw it on the ground and placed her line back into the water. I would then pick up the little fish, jumping about for dear life, and return it to the water. I never let mamma see me do this, however.

Isabella and I were always goggle-eyed at mamma's behavior when she fished. She would get so exited about catching another fish I don't think she ever wondered what happened to the ones that went missing.

On this particular morning we were riding along at a fast pace sitting bumpity-bumpity in mamma's little buggy.

The little red mare was having a good time, too. She raced along with her ears straight up and her tail swishing this way and that. Her bushy tail would almost swipe us in the face – almost, but not quite. So we enjoyed the ride as best we could, knowing full well the horse was not going to let her tail do us any harm.

Suddenly, and without warning, the little horse neighed a loud, frightened scream and stopped dead in its tracks! Mamma, Isabella and I just managed to avoid being thrown out on our heads. As the three of us scrambled to regain our seats, the little red mare stood shaking with fright. Her ears were laid back as if ready for a fight, her eyes huge and glittering. The little horse was evidently terrified. And now, mamma, Isabella and I were not only terrified, but at the mercy of the immobile little mare.

Mamma tried to make the little horse gitty-up, but to no avail. She just stood where she had stopped, trembling.

The road we were traveling was near the river and we had traveled it many times. There was a low place almost immediately ahead of us. Seeing as we couldn't make the horse go forward we decided to get down and see what was frightening her. When we reached the part of the road where it descended, we were amazed. The road was gone! A huge hole appeared where the road had been and water was bubbling up all around.

Then, the most mystifying sight met our eyes. For there were trees walking about in the water! I shall never forget. The leafy limbs of these trees seemed to be reaching out for something to hold onto, but there was nothing, because all the neighboring trees were gone, too!

I'm sure we stood petrified only a short while, but it seemed like forever. As we watched, a lake was forming and more trees appeared. Some of them were small trees, and they, too, seemed to be walking on the water, looking for a place to settle down. Just about now all three of us must have realized the swirling water and walking trees were getting very close and personal. It was then Isabella grabbed mamma and me by the arm in one great motion, yelling, "We'd better get the hell outta here!" And, strange to say, all I could think of at that moment was that I'd never heard Isabella say "hell" before!

With Isabella half dragging us, we reached the buggy. The little red mare was still terrified but after the three of us scrambled in, mamma managed to get the horse and buggy turned around. And she only had to yell "gitty-up" once before the little red mare had us half-way out of the woods!

The little horse was running so fast we had to hold on for dear life, the bumpity-bumpity of our out-bound journey now replaced by the bangity-bang-boom of our return! In fact, as we neared the farm, mamma realized the red mare was not going to stop. So she and Isabella stood up and began screaming and waving, trying to get the attention of any field-hands nearby.

As I look back and remember, I realize we must have been a comical but terrifying sight: a run-away horse and buggy with a white and a black woman waving and screaming, and a little child clinging to its mother somewhere in between! In reality, I was probably too little to be seen. Furthermore, I was crouched on the floor of the buggy, my face hidden in the folds of mother's dress. Scared as I was, I might have been even more scared if I thought I was going to be punished. But on this particular occasion I had the sure knowledge I was innocent of any wrongdoing.

By this time Daddy and most of the men working near enough to hear the screaming came running. And by the time the red mare passed the barn, two young black men had caught up with us, running along either side of the buggy. The poor, frightened horse began to relax. She probably remembered being run down by these boys before!

The two black men assisted mamma and Isabella in getting out of the buggy and I scampered out also. Then mamma and Isabella began breathlessly telling about the huge lake appearing out of nowhere, washing the road away and making the trees rise up and walk on water!!!

I could tell by the expressions on the faces of the men surrounding us they were all thinking, "Miss Ruth's been in the white lightning!" Nobody at first believed us! But it finally dawned on several of them that something out of the ordinary had happened, and soon everyone was running toward the river.

The children were told to stay home and mamma, Isabella, and I had already seen enough, so we just sat on the porch and waited. Meanwhile, the little red mare was eating its hay as if the whole thing was just a bad dream. You could tell she believed, however, for her eyes were still very large.

Later that day, Daddy and the men returned. They all had dazed looks on their faces. They found the large lake alright, and how the road disappeared into the rushing waters. And they saw the trees that burst upon the surface, some swirling about in the center, some moving toward the outer edges desperately attaching themselves to anything that would hold them.

As the years went by, the new lake became a part of the river. The theory of the new lake was that an underground river had been there since prehistoric times. This theory was put forward because of the many odd fish that appeared, never having been seen before. For example, there were little albino fish, but also blind fish that had no eyes. These fish had never existed in our streams and rivers and were very unusual. But once the lake became part of the river, they disappeared and were never seen again.

As a child, I use to wonder about the strange little fish, and what became of them. It bothered me their homes had been disturbed and that they had been freed only to become lost. I hoped their disappearing meant they found their way home – wherever it was!

We heard stories in later years about this type of phenomenon occurring in parts of South Georgia and northern Florida. And my favorite history teacher used to tell us the lands of Georgia and Florida had once been underwater - a part of the Atlantic Ocean. She even predicted they would become part of the ocean again.[14]

All I know is mamma's poor little red mare never would go along the road to that part of the woods again. Nor would I, who tried to have as much horse sense!

---

[14] The Little River and The Withlacoochee in south Georgia (near Valdosta) have peculiar underground limestone caverns which flow in and out rather suddenly. Furthermore, in western Brooks County, there is a phenomenon called "Dry Lake." This lake fills from time to time, also quite suddenly, emptying just as suddenly from underground sources which are thought to be part of a common subterranean system (Letter from Dr. Steve Edmondson to editor, 18 May 2010).

MOUSIE'S GETTING MARRIED!

Everything was changing on the farm. Mousie and I were thirteen, and my sister Claudene and Alice were fourteen. Mousie and Alice, two little black girls who lived on our farm, were Claudene's and my special playmates.

All the children were beginning to notice changes in their interests and their choices of people. And the changes in their bodies were beginning to be noticed, too.

Claudene looked like mamma and Alice looked like her mamma. Poor little me stayed little and skinny. I wanted to bulge a little here and there, but it didn't happen.

As I write this, I am referring to a time almost a hundred years ago. A young girl wasn't told any of the facts of life and she certainly better not ask. So most of us got married not knowing where babies came from. You can only imagine the shock and surprise when my first child was born. Most of us always thought you married, then selected your babies through mail-order, although the person you placed this order with remained a mystery. Of course, after the first child, you usually figured this out.

One day, I noticed Mousie giggling and her eyes were big

and sparkling. And wherever you saw Ed, the young black man who spent the summer with his grandmother, Mousie was not far away.

You may recall from one of my earlier stories Ed was the person who got bit by a rattler while working in the fields. It was Mousie who took care of him. Ed was nearly eighteen, just a boy really, but five years older than Mousie.

It wasn't long before I began noticing Mousie getting a little on the plump side. When I mentioned this to her, she would giggle even more and appear quite happy.

One morning when Mousie seemed especially happy, she whispered she wanted to tell me something. So after breakfast we slipped away from the kitchen and ran down to our special hiding place, a fallen tree extending over the creek. We often went there to get away from everyone and discuss our secrets. Boy! It was a miracle I didn't fall off that log and into the creek when Mousie told me her secret!

"Ed says we're going to have a baby," she told me.

"Well thank the Lord for Ed!" I laughed, "But how does he know?"

"He says that's why I'm getting so rolly-polly," she whispered. "And I've been sleeping with him since the snake bit him. He wanted me to sleep with him 'cause it made the pain go away.'

Despite our general ignorance, both of us knew sleeping with a boy usually had something to do with babies. But Mousie was happy to be having a baby so it didn't matter to her if she learned this after the fact. As for me, I would have wanted to know this ahead of time!

Then a thought struck me. "Mousie," I said, "you're supposed to be married before the baby comes." With this, her eyes grew bigger. "But I ain't married!" she said.

"But you can be - you and Ed can get married! Then you can live in the little house down by the creek." I reminded her about the little house the Bruces lived in before they returned to New York City.

I was so excited, I was saying just about anything. But I realized we would first have to talk to Ed about the marriage and also to Daddy about the house.

"Then we'll have to tell your mamma," I said.

"Mamma already knows. In fact, she asked me the other day when I was going to move in with Ed."

Wow! I never would have imagined her mother being so broad-minded. Had it been my mother, I would have been skinned alive! So I told Mousie we had done enough talking for the day and would meet again on the morrow. After that, we both ran home.

What were Mousie and I going to do? To my way of thinking, Mousie should be getting married. But I knew very well it was not that important to her. A hundred years ago, it was usual for most poor people, black or white, not to get married. The few dollars needed for a license and wedding dress was the determining factor, I think. Then too, preachers were scarce. But regardless, all the black people on our farm were committed to each other and lived together all their lives. Even when times had changed and the blacks had a nice little church of their own - one that still stands today.[15] I know they had funerals there but I don't recall any marriages.

When Mousie and I had our first opportunity, we hurried back to the fallen tree across the creek. Mousie was jubilant as she told me Ed agreed to get married. "Praise the Lord!" I thought, "That takes care of that." But little did I realize there was so much more to it than that! For one thing, I knew I would need to talk to mamma into helping us. I say I would need to talk mamma into this because I knew she would think it a silly waste of time. Her thought would be, "Mousie is pregnant - so what?!"

---

[15] 1994.

So the next morning after breakfast I gathered up all my courage and spoke to mother in my most confident, imposing manner. "Mamma, I want you to help me make Mousie a wedding dress. And I also want you to help me make a braidsmaid's dress for Alice."

As always, mamma was busy with something, but had a ready answer, nonetheless. "Juanita, do you realize how much the material for those two dresses would cost?"

"Yes," I told her, "but I'll get Uncle Willis to help."

Uncle Willis had a dry-goods store in Marian. We bought material from him, so I intended to ask his assistance. He could sell us material for the two dresses at a discount or maybe even give us what we needed. Uncle Willis was a good, kind man who passed away some time ago. But he lived to a ripe old age and is survived by his two daughters.

Anyway, I went to Uncle Willis' country store and found him in the back putting up stock.

"Uncle Willis," I called, "I need your help."

He immediately came down off the ladder he was using and stood before me.

"My! My! I thought, "He sure is a big man!"

But when he smiled his kind, caring smile, I knew he would help me. So I told him my problem involving eight yards of pretty material needed to make dresses for both Mousie and Alice. And as it turned out, he liked the idea. He saw the importance of Mousie getting married. So he gave me four yards of beautiful white material with lace and ribbon for Mousie's wedding dress, and four yards of beautiful pink material for Alice's dress. He also offered materials for the new baby but I told him everyone on the place was already working on baby clothes.

All the new babies on our farm started their lives with flour-sack clothes. Back then, our baking flour came in soft cotton sacks, and these were saved for new babies' clothing and diapers.

When I reached home with the material Uncle Willis gave me, I marched inside, then up the stairs to the sewing room. I laid the material on the cutting table and went in search of mamma. Gosh, was I scared! I just knew mamma would either be thrilled when she saw the lovely material for the dresses or she would kill me! I have seen her explode with such force when she was angry, the rafters shook. But she just <u>had</u> to help me make those dresses! My sewing skills were not good enough. And I wanted those dresses as perfect as possible.

I did not have to go far to find mamma. She came bounding up the stairs shouting "Young lady!" loud enough to bring the house down. "Young lady" was the expression used for all little girls on our farm just before they were given a switching that was supposed to last a lifetime. Because of this, I never got excited when hearing people brag about gallberry honey. The honey is made from berries picked from the gallberry bush. And the switches from this plant are so tough you can whip a whole family with just one of them!

So when mamma shouted "Young lady!" I braced for the gallberry switch. But mamma glanced down at the material on the cutting board and curiosity got the better of her. Or was it her love of beautiful things? She carefully raised the lovely fabric, and held it between herself and the window. This act always revealed the quality of a material and mamma knew good material. She was an expert seamstress.

When any of the family needed a special dress, mamma would go to the only fashion shop in Valdosta and examine the dress she wanted to copy. The sales girls thought she was looking to buy but we knew she wasn't. We knew she would go back home, take a piece of newspaper and cut a pattern like the dress she saw in the shop. And more often than not, by the time she had finished, the dress would turn out better than the one in the store.

I could see by the intense expression on mamma's face, as she turned the material this way and that, she was already planning Mousie's dress!

Boy! Did things move fast after that. Within a few days, both the white and pink dresses were finished and they looked absolutely beautiful on Mousie and Alice.

Most of the mothers had go-to-meeting clothes they wore to church, and from these they began choosing the dresses they would wear to Mousie's wedding. Most adult farm people in fact, both black and white, had at least one set of clothes for special occasions. So it wasn't a big problem to dress for a wedding.

The corsages, however, were a different matter. These would have to be made. Fortunately, we had plenty of flowers in the yards and the woodlands. So by gathering and arranging these flowers we could make the corsages the evening before the wedding.

A reception after the wedding – something I wanted – would be no problem either. Not the food part, anyway. Isabella and Sugar were excellent cooks, as were most of the people who lived on the farm. Preparing a large and sumptuous meal for a hundred or so guests was easy to arrange.

Something that wasn't was how to prepare the church. Nobody, but nobody believed in decorating a church for any reason, even for funerals. I don't know the true reason for this, but it seems most people thought God could not find us if we did not keep things uncluttered. So rather than have someone feel we were desecrating the house of the Lord, there would be nothing out of the ordinary and certainly no decorating.

Just like the dresses, once mamma got involved with the wedding arrangements, things started moving rather quickly. She began by helping all the black women choose their best dresses and if anything needed fixing, such as a hem or a seam or what have you, she was right there to do it. And when she had finished with all the black folk and felt everyone would be as beautiful as possible, she started in on our family.

By now, word had spread about Mousie and Ed's marriage. People, both black and white, began dropping by to ask if they could come.

Mousie was usually in the kitchen helping with the baking and other chores, so we would call her to give permission for those wanting to come. But soon I noticed Mousie was getting very quiet and didn't seem to be as happy as the day wore on. So finally I got her away from the noise and confusion as I knew something was wrong.

"What's the matter, Mousie?" I asked as we reached our special place. "Are you tired? Perhaps you've been working too hard."

Her huge eyes began spilling over with tears.

"I ain't seen Ed all day," she said. "I think he's gone!"

"I'll kill that no good for nothing!" I raged in my mind. "I'll just kill him!" But to Mousie I said, "I'm sure he isn't gone. I'll go down and talk with his Granny."

When I reached Ed's Granny's house, she came out to greet me with the happiest smile on her face, thanking me for helping Mousie and Ed. There was no doubt she was happy about their getting married. When I asked, she told me Ed had gone to his mother's to get a ring she had been saving. Apparently, Ed's mother was hopeful he would someday get married and had promised this ring should he ever find a wife.

Ed's mother lived about fifty miles away. Granny said he would not be back till morning as he had to walk there and back. So now I knew about Ed but could not tell Mousie for fear of giving away his secret.

Next morning, the day before the wedding, Ed returned. Mousie was smiling again even though Ed wouldn't tell her where he'd been.

This was the day everyone who wanted a corsage had to

get busy. As I roamed the fields gathering flowers, I found almost every female on the place out gathering flowers too. We were soon joined by a big flock of whooping cranes that flew in, landing on the nearby pond. They were busily splashing around in the water for the most part but seemed to be watching us flower-gatherers as they did.

The whooping crane is a beautiful, large white or light gray bird with long legs. They often waded in the water and fished. If you walked up on one while it was fishing it would fix its intelligent eyes on you and begin speaking. Or so it seemed. People would say, "The whooping crane called my name!" and it gave a feeling of importance to think this magnificent bird knew you personally. Sadly, I am told this great white bird is now becoming extinct.

On this particular day, however, the flower-gatherers did not take time to converse with the whooping cranes. We all kept working until we were certain we had enough flowers for our corsages. The rest of the day was then given over to actually making them.

So there I was making corsages, when I looked up to see an elderly black couple from an adjoining farm walk into the yard, the man and his wife each bringing a kitchen chair. Then and only then did I realize I had forgotten house-keeping furniture for Mousie and Ed. How stupid of me! Daddy had given permission for the couple to live in the little house by the creek, but I had overlooked the fact they would need furniture!

Thankfully, there were those who understood, this couple for instance, and others. Many of the blacks on our farm shared what they had with the young couple.

As I think on it now, 'tis strange I should have realized the need for dresses, flowers, and food, even the house down by the creek, but not the furniture!

Mousie told us which preacher would perform the wedding ceremony and also that there would be two ladies who were going to sing. But she never said anything about furniture, so

I suppose it was her family and friends who quietly furnished the creek-house.

Everything was moving along wonderfully and even though I hadn't slept for a whole week, I was very happy. I was sure this wedding was going to be something for the whole world, my world anyway, to remember. But all things considered, I wasn't sure I ever wanted to plan another wedding!!! It was so much work, and I was exhausted.

The next day, several hours before daylight, the whole place was already buzzing with excitement. When I woke up around four, a pleasant aroma told me breakfast was ready even at this early hour. The wedding was to be held at eleven, and from the look of things, everyone was hard at work making sure all would be ready. The reception dinner was being prepared by Isabella and Sugar, both of whom looked like they had been up all night. But what astonished me most was seeing mamma cooking breakfast. I couldn't believe my eyes!

Mamma was the daughter of a Methodist preacher and the granddaughter of a hard-shell preacher. So she was brought up knowing the importance of food. I heard her say many times, "Our spring-house was always well stocked with good things to eat," and then she would laughingly add, "In fact, papa stayed in the spring-house when he came off the circuit." "The circuit" referred to his preaching trips.

So mamma knew how to cook but she didn't like to cook if she didn't have to. Mousie's wedding proved to be one of those special occasions when she simply had to!

By the time everyone had finished breakfast, the sun was coming up over the trees. My sister Sarah and I walked out into the yard just in time to see the sun blotted out by another big flock of whooping cranes looking for a place to land. They came swooping in, just missing our heads as they converged on the pond and surrounding area.

Some of the birds were talking among themselves, while

others were letting out great big whooping sounds to express their happiness.

It was then my imagination got the better of me. "Some of those birds are calling my name!" I yelled to my sister. But Sarah yelled back, "No they're not - they're calling <u>my</u> name, you idiot! They're saying 'Sarah' not 'Juanita.' Can't you hear them?!"

I suppose Sarah and I yelling at each other made the birds uneasy and they soon took off together in a huge cloud of dust, still talking and whooping. Some might have said "goodbye," but they definitely didn't call Sarah's name!

As I entered the house after watching the whooping cranes fly away, I thought to myself, "This is going to be a good day, a day I shall never forget. Not only is it Mousie's wedding day but the day the whooping crane called <u>my</u> name!"

We soon began readying ourselves for the wedding, for everyone wanted to get to church early in order to have a front row seat. I was amazed to find everyone from our farm, but also people we knew from neighboring farms, so dressed-up. They were so well dressed we hardly recognized them.

Ed, whom we usually saw in field clothes, had on a very nice suit. And, of course, Mousie and Alice in their new white and pink dresses looked simply stunning!

The wedding began promptly, with beautiful organ music and the two girls who had volunteered to sing soon joining in. They sang so wonderfully everyone was in tears by the time the preacher started speaking. He gave the eulogy but the service was shortened somewhat by the fact Ed had already given Mousie his mother's ring. So the couple was pronounced "man and wife," and the two girls, as well as the whole congregation, broke into song. Tears were again flowing everywhere.

Then somebody grabbed the bride and groom and brought them back to the farm where most of the people were already gathered. And everyone - visitors, guests, farm workers, bride and groom - enjoyed the great feast Isabella and Sugar had been preparing all through the week.

I felt great and all puffed up with pride. I believed I had done it all, and congratulated myself accordingly. "And why shouldn't I be proud?" After all, I was only thirteen!

THE TARANTULA
THAT HAD A FACE[16]

It was a known fact throughout the neighborhood I did not allow harm to any animal. I taught my three sons that every living creature was created for a purpose. And unless that creature was about to harm you - be it a snake, spider, or the guy next door - you did not kill it, or him. So ants, snakes, and people were fairly safe at our house.

Buddy, my number two son, took this edict seriously. I remember, for instance, the time he discovered a huge tarantula on a load of bananas while working his summer job with a wholesale grocer.

Buddy had never seen a spider so large. But he knew what his mother had taught him, so rather than kill the tarantula, he put it in a large glass jar and brought it home.

I am sure he questioned what I'd do when I saw this huge, unsightly creature. "Will she make me squash him?" he might have wondered. For surely, here was a creature for which I might change my mind.

---

[16] Note to the reader: this and the final story were episodes later in Ms. Collins' life when she had become a wife and mother. Given Buddy's birth circa 1940, it is estimated this episode occurred in the late 1940's or very early 50's.

As Buddy handed me the jar, I could tell he was nervous.

Admittedly, I did wonder what to do with the spider. He was gigantic! He was so large, his body covered the entire bottom and his legs spread out along the sides.

I rotated the jar to get a better look. Although about the ugliest creature I had ever seen, I sensed he was intelligent, for he indeed had a face, with very bright eyes that never left me. When I moved from side to side, the spider did not move, but his eyes did.

There was probably nothing this spider feared, being so big and ugly. His face seemed almost human. But although fearsome, his expression at times reminded me of a frightened child.

"He is a perfect creation. But what is he created for?"

As word got around about the spider Buddy had brought home, people from the neighborhood came by to see it. Looking at it up close, they "oh'd" and "aw'd," then instinctively backed away in fear. "That's the ugliest creature I've ever seen," they would say. "Why don't you kill it?" But I would again explain my policy we didn't kill anything that didn't harm you. "Maybe so, but if he should ever escape..." And so forth. I had to admit, the thought of the spider getting loose bothered me. I suppose under those circumstances we would be in peril and might have to kill it.

As I watched the spider watch me, a feeling of protective kindness crept over me. I knew I'd have to figure out a way to feed him. "What does he eat?," I wondered. "Well, he came into this country on a boat-load of bananas - maybe he eats bananas!"

So for three days I tried feeding him bananas, insects and so forth. But he wouldn't eat anything. All he would do is lie on his belly and follow me with his eyes.

After three days, it was obvious he was loosing weight. He got smaller and smaller, but his eyes seemed to get larger, making his face look very sad. Those large eyes kept looking at me and I imagined he was begging for help. It was obvious he must be hungry.

About this time I named him "Trangy" - and there went my heart! Buddy was fond of him too, and wanted to keep him as a pet. But despite everything I did, poor Trangy would not eat. He just kept getting smaller and smaller. So it became obvious there was only one thing to do. Rather than let him starve, I would set him free. It was a hard decision, for I had grown close to Trangy and knew Buddy had too. Nevertheless, one day when Buddy was at work, I took the jar and carried Trangy to the pasture behind our house. Trangy moved very little, but kept himself positioned so as to see what I was up to. And I believe he understood what I was going to do.

I placed the jar on its side and removed the lid. I also put a banana on the grass nearby, hoping, once free, he might finally eat. But when I left him there and said "good-bye," naively expecting him to wave "farewell," he merely sat in the jar and wouldn't budge. Silently I understood, and went back to the house to leave him alone.

After reaching the house, I waited as long as I could. But after a few moments I ran back to the pasture to see if Trangy was still there. As I approached the jar I stopped. For I seemed to already know, my eyes instantly filling with tears of joy and sadness: Trangy was gone!

With a happy heart, I returned to the house and later that evening told Buddy. "There was nothing more we could do for Trangy, so I set him free." Buddy was naturally disappointed. He was still just a young boy, so I tried to explain. I told him there was more to letting people and animals live, they also needed their freedom.

"Someday, when it is your turn, I hope to have this same courage for you."

LAST TRIP THROUGH GEORGIA[17]

A few days ago, I found myself in Waycross Georgia, land of mystery and "the trembling Earth." Okefinoke Swamp, an area about seven hundred square miles in Southeast Georgia and Northeast Florida, snaked along beside me as I searched for the road that would lead me to Valdosta.[18]

As I drove along, my mind went back to the first time I visited this spectacular area. I remember the tall, stalwart Indian who was telling us about the Great Swamp. He told us, "It was the Indian who gave the swamp its name. We called it 'Land of the Trembling Earth' many moons before the white man came."

As we waited for our guide and the boat that would take us through the swamp, the Indian told us several stories about the area and the people who made their homes there.

---

[17] Ms. Collins' very last trip through Georgia occurred November of 2000 when she revisited her cousin, Sophronia Edmondson, and the building that was once Morven High School.

[18] Okefinoke Swamp, according to the 1944 edition of Encyclopedia Americana, occupies nearly all of Charlton County, and parts of Ware and Clinch Counties, Georgia, extending into Baker County, Florida. Alligators and moccasins inhabit this swamp in large numbers.

"I might go home tonight and find the 'trembling Earth' has swallowed up everything I have." Seeing how we children were bug-eyed with fright, he readily continued.

"Once I left my number two wife and two good coon hounds to go fishing. My number two wife and the two hounds needed food. Sometimes we would catch plenty of fish but sometimes the alligators took over the good fishing places and we had to settle for a baby alligator if we could catch one." The Indian was getting a big kick out of scaring us half to death. As he spoke, I watched the silent, slowly moving water but didn't see any movement or upheaval. Waters where alligators lived, even baby alligators, should be turbulent, so I began to feel he was putting us on.

"When I got to where my home was supposed to be, everything was gone. The huge log that had lain beside my lean-to for years was quietly edging down and pulling everything with it... For miles I could see the moving, trembling surface of the swamp. I was filled with terror as tree tops waved to me on their way down, leaving the trembling Earth to cover their leafy tops."

I, being a little girl, was more interested in what happened to the number two wife and dogs. I now scanned the swamp in abject terror. I don't know if it was the power of suggestion but by now I think I saw snakes wrapped around the swaying trees. And I also saw the thick moving water roll up and expose two alligators either playing, fighting, or mating!

This trip to Okefinoke Swamp occurred many years ago. There were no walk-ways then. But many people knew their way through the swamp and would often disappear for months, especially if they ran afoul of the law. Many moon-shiners, I am told, moved their liquor-making operations there. One of these moon-shiners was asked how he lived among the gators. The old fellow replied with a grin, "I keep 'em drunk!"

Today, as I drove along the perimeter of the swamp, I noticed walk-ways built through the area. And it now seemed there was less water and fewer mysteries. Obviously, there are many factors that go into land management and the preservation of areas such as the Okefinoke and I suppose the costs prevented the states of Georgia and Florida from keeping the swamp as it was.

As I passed along, my mind went back to the beautiful birds that were a part of the swamp. Are they still there? And what about the other animals, the many snakes for instance, that helped balance the ecology in South Georgia. Are they still there? Was the alligator completely destroyed before it became a protected species? Does anyone still hear the Bull Alligator bellow for his mate?

These are some of the thoughts that ran through my mind as I left the Okefinoke area. As I drove along, I recalled the guide we had waited for that day never arrived and the Indian never did tell us what happened to his number two wife and dogs.

My family owned a farm just north of Valdosta and we often explored the area. We heard stories of people being found with little children on the floating islands of the "trembling Earth." So maybe number two wife and the two hounds were eventually found on one of these islands.

As I reached the Valdosta exit, I decided not to take it. I have visited Valdosta several times in the past two years due to illness in my family. And though I didn't visit it on this occasion, I must say I was happily impressed with the growth and stability of this, my most favorite Georgia city.

Valdosta, and Waycross too, are cities of intrigue and history. And my daughter-in-law and I were pleased to know they still practice the old rites of politeness and proper behavior. Not so long ago, she & I were lost in the older part of Valdosta. Seeing a utility truck, I pulled alongside and asked directions. The young man gave us detailed instructions and said we should not have any trouble. I thanked him and said, "I sure hope not sir, or you will have to take us home with you!" He looked startled for a moment, then said with a smile, "Follow me ladies. I'll take you where you want to go!"

I also once loved Atlanta but haven't visited this city in a long while. I pass through by necessity but usually put my cruise control on ninety and close my eyes! Truly, however, Atlanta is a marvel to behold. I think it is fast becoming the hub of the whole world. It is a huge metropolis, home to many of our largest industries, and I'm told if you expect to get to heaven, you've got to fly through Atlanta first!

As I bypassed Valdosta, I drove my car toward the Pauline Section of South Georgia. This brought me to my old home area. I passed through Morven, Barney and on through Adel to Interstate-75 North. All these small towns were once home to me. Then there was Hahira, Georgia where all the cutest boys lived. But I must not forget Quitman. There, I found my future husband, a handsome giant if ever there was one![19]

I think the way we lived, the way we loved and helped each other to have a good quality of life, has never been told in its entirety. I remember how we worked our farm land together, whole families of blacks and whites on all the farms I knew. None of us, black or white, had any money. I don't think we needed any. We had everything.

Most South Georgia farms, as far as I knew, were able to take care of their own needs. For instance, we had a "Granny Woman" who cared for everyone. If you broke your arm, she set it for you. If you busted your head, she sewed it up. She also delivered all the babies, both black and white, born on our farm. And I don't think she ever died, just kept on and on, doing her job.

---

[19] Hazel Juanita Winters married Wilbur G. Collins December 26, 1937. A diesel engineer by trade, he would later help Mrs. Collins run Grandview Lodge in Waynesville, N.C. Mr. Collins passed away in 1980.

As I drove along, all these things ran helter-skelter through my mind. I already knew that when I reached the area where our farm spread out through the lakes and ponds, the river and many acres of land, there would be nothing there. The old farmhouse that housed about twenty-five or thirty of us had been torn down a long time ago. But I liked to go back and walk down near the spring that ran north. Doing this always reminded me of the disagreement I once had with Mr. Moore, our school principal. Not that I return to remember this disagreement. For in general I enjoy my memories of the old man, not least of which because he allowed a small child to disagree with him. One day in class he made the statement all running water in Georgia flowed south. I knew immediately this statement was wrong. We had a spring branch on our farm that ran north. So I raised my hand and said "Sir, you are wrong. Our spring branch flows north." I could tell Mr. Moore was shocked. In our day, no student contradicted a teacher, parent or any other adult. Mr. Moore was dumbfounded at first, but then he smiled. "Juanita, if you can prove me wrong I'd like for you to do so." He paused again, then pointed his finger at me. "But until you do, all running water in Georgia runs south!"

That night at supper, I told my grandpa what happened at school. My mother's reaction was to reprimand me for un-lady like behavior. My father, who was accustomed to not saying anything, remained silent. But Grandpa Bill said, "Juanita, invite Mr. and Mrs. Moore to have supper with us tomorrow night and we'll show him the flowing water that runs north."

Mr. Moore came, ate supper, saw the spring branch flowing north and patted me on the head.

Mr. Moore taught me the basics of learning while teaching at our little school in Morven, which incidentally, still stands today.[20] I never saw him refuse to listen to a child who spoke

---

[20] The original building has since been converted to Morven City Hall.

up in class. A child was never ridiculed for his ideas. Mr. Moore taught me to think. His specialty was Math. As he stood at the blackboard with chalk in hand he would tell us that if we learned to add, subtract and multiply, we had the key to success in any field. I'm sure he was right. I became something of a whiz in Math and can add up the Bridge score of someone else's hand being held upside down form across the Bridge table. And I can do this even while the Bridge player holding the cards gives up trying to add their own score! Often, when I do this, I think of Mr. Moore.

But I'm afraid the one-two, one-two of the dance step doesn't get to my feet. So I didn't choose dancing as a career.

On this day, after visiting with my old Math teacher in memory, I found myself pulling into the parking area of the Pauline Baptist Church not far from our old homestead. It was beautifully kept as the Black Church in the area, but as I looked at other churches still standing these past hundred years, I wondered where all the people were? The miles and miles of farms and the people who worked these farms seemed to be gone, too. I remember when I was a young girl, my family and the young black people on our farm used to gather on the front porch and sing. Soon thereafter, people, both black and white, came walking from everywhere and joined in the singing.[21] I did not see a living soul as I came into the area. If I should start singing, would they come?

After searching the neighborhood for memories of yesterday, I drove about a mile down the road and parked my car where the old oak trees used to shade our porch and front yard. This was a favorite spot for all the farm children to come and play. The huge trunks of the old oak trees still stood but everything else was gone. The old house, the water well that was dug at

---

[21] Booth Tarkington's "The Gentleman from Indiana" (1899) gives reason to believe singing and socializing on front porches was once a northern pastime as well.

the end of the porch near where the Cooling Board was located, all this was long gone. But I remembered!

I walked down to the hickory nut orchard and found the four clay mounds, or just a shadow of them, still there. It's strange, by modern standards today, that the mounds were never dug up to see if anyone was buried there. Mousie and Alice, the two little black girls I played with when I was growing up, told us Indians were buried there before white people came from England to settle Georgia. But that's all I ever heard anyone say about the mounds.

As I walked over the rich black earth where I once picked cotton with Mousie and Alice, I realized I would probably never come this way again. There is much I want to explore in Georgia but haven't quite finished with the South Georgia I knew. For instance, there are the remains of a huge house built on the river just north of Valdosta. When last I saw it, the beautiful columns were still there but the river had taken its toll. It was my great-grandfather's house.[22] The river ran through his plantation. There was great-grandpa, great-grandma and about fifteen children. There was Ol' Man Oss (my grandfather), Aunt Sis, Aunt Joe, Aunt Puss and several other relations that died before I knew them. Due to the history of that house, I think I must be related to almost everyone in South Georgia!

The stories of Georgia's struggle to become the great state she is are doubtless recorded in the history books. But they are also and especially recorded in the minds of the many people who lived that struggle. Everywhere you look, there are signs of greatness and achievement!

Continuing my walk through the land that had once been our family farm, I noted a little house across the field, and buildings with machinery scattered about. This was near the

---

[22] William Edmondson (1849 – 1930), aka "Grandpa Bill," mentioned in several earlier stories.

spring branch that mysteriously flowed north. It made me happy to see people were still farming the land.

A lady came out on the porch of the house as I approached. She did not look like a farmer in the old sense, certainly not like we looked after a hard day's work in the fields. I don't suppose anyone sees a woman plowing with a mule anymore!

She invited me to sit on the steps with her and talk a spell. As we did, I asked her many questions I had wanted to ask someone who still lived here. "Do you ever hear the scream of the wildcat?" "Do you ever see the little brown bear?" "Do you ever hear the bellow of the alligator?" "Do you know where the rattlesnake sleeps at night?" To this last question, my listener looked startled. "You <u>do</u> know that rattlesnakes like to sleep in warm places, don't you?" The woman's eyes got bigger and bigger. She looked at me like a frightened deer. "I've never heard of these things," she said.

"These are the animals that frequented our farms, or used to, when I lived here many years ago," I told her. "But they probably don't anymore" I added, seeing her discomfort. With that I bid her goodbye and wished her good luck, telling how pleased I was she and her husband were making the farm productive again.

As I walked back to my car, memory again reminded me about the Georgia I knew as a little girl. Our little train, the "Ol' South Georgia," was brought before my eyes. I could see it on the verge of crossing our land.

The cross-ties on the tracks would start bouncing, the little train would sway from side-to-side, and right on the dot at eleven o'clock she pulled onto our farm, her whistle shrieking three times. All the little black and white cotton-pickers would let out a yell and drop their cotton sacks, running all the way back to the kitchen for their dinners of black-eyed peas, turnip greens, cornbread and gallons of buttermilk!

Afterward, everyone was free to run down to the clear, lazy

river and swim and play until two o'clock. There we would frolic and splash and laugh until it was time to go back to the cotton patch to pick more cotton until the sun went down behind the trees.

Many of these memories of the "Ol' South Georgia" float before my eyes. There was a trestle over the creek on our land. As the train left our farm over the trestle she always sounded her shrill whistle one last time.

I believe there was someone who used to sing, "The freight train whistle taught me how to cry." Well, our freight train whistle taught us how to jump for joy whenever we heard it. But we were never allowed to play near, or on, the trestle. Never mind that it was a necessary part of the railroad track that crossed the creek that crossed our land. Truth is, for some reason, the deadly coral snake loved the trestle, too. They reared their young under the cross-ties. Fortunately, the bright colors of the coral snake made it hard for them to hide from us. But still our elders didn't want us taking any chances. For we were taught: "The cotton-mouth moccasin might kill you if he bites you, the rattlesnake will probably kill you if he bites you, but the coral snake will definitely kill you if he bites you!" Therefore, all the children on our farm took their mothers seriously when they told us not to play on the trestle. Even in modern times, I believe there is anti-venom for all snake bites in Georgia except that of the coral. In short, we didn't play on the trestle!

I suppose the "South Georgia" was the highlight of the day for all the rural people whose land it crossed. The little train came rambling through the farm lands shrieking "Hello!" to everyone and "Goodbye!" in like manner. All the young girls on the farms the little train passed over would run down to the track hoping a handsome young engineer was at the controls that day. They waved and shouted happily until the train was out of sight. Come to think of it, they waved and shouted happily even if somebody's grandpa was driving the train!

As I sat in my car and let my imagination run in all directions, I again became a little girl of five or six. Sometimes when I did this, I even let my mind take me back to the day I learned to walk.

South Georgia was a happy place when I was growing up. I do not recall being afraid of anything. If you were an achiever you had the encouragement of everyone. And if you were not an achiever, you still had the encouragement of everyone. The fact we loved the black families that were a part of our farm and they loved us meant so much to me over the years. This is something I shall always remember.

But my memory also tells me I was a mean little devil. Just like my sister Claudene, I was always getting into scrapes. But aside from sheer meanness, I recall if we did not think fast and stay on our feet, something or someone, was always ready to pull the world out from under us!

I cranked my car and returned to the area where our family home had stood for many years. I said "goodbye" to all the faces I could no longer see and the lifestyle that is no more.

It is so good to be able to appreciate the opportunities we had to help mold the great state of Georgia. I think my mother was most proud of a certificate given her by Franklin Delano Roosevelt, President of the United States. The Second World War was ending. The country was hungry. The President asked that everyone who had farms grow food. "Our people are starving," he said.[23]

My mother was a widow with a farm she had quit trying to farm after father died. She put the farm back into operation and produced thousands of pounds of food, earning a special award and a certificate of thanks from the President. This too, I shall always remember!

As I left South Georgia and drove through middle and north Georgia, my mind would not set me free. I traveled with an awareness of all the precious moments of our history. I know that many events in our world just happen and many are also destined to happen. This is how it was with Georgia. The early settlers laid the foundation for our great State with hard work and grateful hearts.

As I passed through Atlanta, I didn't pray this time but sang, "Georgia Land, Dear Georgia Land!" But in the midst of this rejoicing I was reminded how our history is sometimes fraught with individual sadness. My bliss was soon cut short by an unexpected call. My youngest sister, "Little Sarah," had just passed away.

FINIS

---

[23] Samuel Goldwyn Productions' "The Best Years of Our Lives" (1946), lends credence to this situation in a scene where bank representative Al Stephenson (Frederick March) interviews a sharecropper named "Novak" who hopes to get a farm loan by citing this same U.S. and world food shortage. It is generally conceded, however, U.S. W.W. II food shortages were minimal compared with other combatant nations.

Printed in the United States
By Bookmasters